"A very timely book for a very isolated culture. Amy Lively offers practical help and guidance in the neglected practice of hospitality."

—Dr. Dennis Rainey,
president, FamilyLife

"This ministry is changing lives in neighborhoods all over the communities that we serve. Amy has followed God's leading into an untapped area of people that need Jesus. What a simple idea of reaching out to your neighborhood—the area that God placed you in for His purposes and Kingdom. Amy's ideas and excellent resources have offered a no-excuse zone for this ministry. The Lord said, 'Love me and love your neighbor.' He chose Amy to show us the way. Thank you for this amazing resource! Now let's go make disciples!"

—Chrissy Dunham,
director of women's ministry at
Prestonwood Baptist Church, Plano, Texas

"Amy knows God has given each of us a corner of the world to share the love of Jesus and the hope found in His Word. Her book equips women, spiritually and practically, to answer this call and open their hearts and homes to friends and neighbors."

—Wendy Blight,
Proverbs 31 Ministries speaker and author

"Have you longed to reach out in your neighborhood but feel paralyzed by doubts and fears? Me too! Amy's practical advice from her own experiences gives the equipping 'how to' as well as the inspirational 'want to.' She motivates you to push past the obstacles and live Jesus' command to love our neighbors."

—Amy Carroll,
Proverbs 31 Ministries speaker and author

"I am a product of one neighbor walking across a front yard and stepping into the life of another neighbor. Amy's brilliant approach to engaging our neighbors is natural, fun, and life-changing! She provides every single thing you will need, including courage. This book and practice is a *must* for everyone desiring to honor and obey the Lord."

—Debbie Stuart,
church and leadership development director,
Women of Faith

"Amy gets it—we want to connect with our neighbors without being that neighbor (you know, the one who makes you want to screen their calls and dim the lights when you see them coming up the driveway). In *How to Love Your Neighbor Without Being Weird* to really connect with those who live around us

but with a heart toward real relationships. A must-read for anyone who believes that 'Love thy neighbor' really starts at your front door."

—Kathi Lipp,
coauthor of *The Cure for the Perfect Life*
and author of *The Husband Project*

"With hundreds of friends on social media, why are we so lonely? In her amazing book, *How to Love Your Neighbor Without Being Weird*, Amy Lively identifies the heart-need for deep connection that's not being met through a screen and offers a simple solution: Actually meet the people who live near you. Amy's openness to share her successes and failures at reaching out will inspire you to try it yourself. If you still wonder how, Amy has packed the book with creative and practical ways to love those God has called our 'neighbor.'"

—Glynnis Whitwer,
author of *I Used to Be So Organized* and *Everyday Confetti*,
executive director of communications, Proverbs 31 Ministries

"Practical and insightful, *How to Love Your Neighbor Without Being Weird* is a fresh reminder of God's desire for us to love our neighbors in the midst of our everyday lives. Amy shows us step-by-step how to conquer our fears, connect with our neighbors, and have fun too! Highly recommend!"

—Cindy Bultema,
speaker, Bible teacher, and author of *Red Hot Faith*

"What does 'love your neighbor as yourself' really mean? In this book, *How to Love Your Neighbor Without Being Weird*, Amy Lively will give you the tips, tools, and techniques you need to love your neighbor in your own unique way. Whether you know the names of every person on your street, or couldn't pick them out in a lineup, you will learn how to develop a relationship and, ultimately, share Jesus with them. Amy's book is a practical and encouraging tool to use as you are trying to apply God's commandments to your life."

—Jennifer Rothschild,
author of *Lessons I Learned in the Dark*; *Self Talk, Soul Talk*;
and *God Is Just Not Fair: Finding Hope When Life
Doesn't Make Sense*; founder of Fresh Grounded Faith events
and womensministry.net

"I don't know when I've been more excited about a book or when I've agreed with an author with more enthusiasm. Amy's passion for her neighbors is catching. I hope her stories will grab your heart and motivate you as much as they have me. She really understands what 'heavenly hospitality' is and shows the reader how to practice it as well."

—Nan McCullough, Entertaining For Eternity

# How to Love Your Neighbor

## without being weird

# AMY LIVELY

BETHANY HOUSE PUBLISHERS
a division of Baker Publishing Group
Minneapolis, Minnesota

Published by Bethany House Publishers
11400 Hampshire Avenue South
Bloomington, Minnesota 55438
www.bethanyhouse.com

Bethany House Publishers is a division of
Baker Publishing Group, Grand Rapids, Michigan

Printed in the United States of America

Library of Congress Cataloging-in-Publication Data
Lively, Amy.
    How to love your neighbor without being weird / Amy Lively.
        pages cm
    Includes bibliographical references.
    Summary: "Encouragement and hands-on ideas for Christian women who want to meet their neighbors and build relationships within their communities"— Provided by publisher.
        ISBN 978-0-7642-1700-5 (pbk. : alk. paper) 1. Christian women. 2. Love— Religious aspects—Christianity. I. Title.
    BR1713.L58 2015
    248.8′43—dc23                                                          2014045831

Cover design by Rob Williams, InsideOutCreativeArts

Author is represented by Books & Such Literary Agency.

15  16  17  18  19  20  21          7  6  5  4  3  2  1

In keeping with biblical principles of creation stewardship, Baker Publishing Group advocates the responsible use of our natural resources. As a member of the Green Press Initiative, our company uses recycled paper when possible. The text paper of this book is composed in part of post-consumer waste.

green
press
INITIATIVE

*To Bob—*
*who represents all my neighbors*
*who opened their homes to me*
*and graciously came into mine.*

# Contents

# Acknowledgments

Much love and many thanks to the following:

David, who happily retreats to his office when I fill our home with women and believes in me more than I believe in myself.

Emma, I can't wait to read the story God is writing in your life. Love you, babe.

Mom and Dad, who put a sticker on my bedroom door that said "Be all you can be," and always believed I'd be a writer.

Ron and Marilyn and my Life Church family, who equipped me for ministry then released me to actually do it.

My gGg's—Michelle, kindred spirit who prayed our friendship into existence; Heather and her ruthless red pen; and Amy, Cindy, Debbie, Lisa, Elizabeth, Judy, Vicky, and Wendy—who have prayed for you readers and for me without ceasing.

Proverbs 31 Ministries, who whispered the words *neighborhood Bible study* into my heart, then taught me how to follow my dreams.

Neighbors who opened their doors, offered a smile, and extended their kindness—even when caught off guard by a stranger at the door.

Jesus Christ, who knew exactly what would happen when we moved into this big, ugly house. Be glorified, Lord, be glorified.

# Introduction

I wanted to love my neighbor, but I didn't know how.

I felt guilty about Christ's command to love my neighbor, but I didn't even *know* most of the people living around me. Some of my neighbors were scary (like the ones who named their dog Demon), and some were rude (like the ones who didn't answer the door when I delivered a welcome basket). Sure, most of them were quite nice—but some of them were intimidating, and others were uninteresting.

Trouble was, I couldn't find an exception clause in the second-greatest commandment (trust me, I looked *hard*)—

> "You must love the Lord your God with all your heart, all your soul, and all your mind." This is the first and greatest commandment. A second is equally important: "Love your neighbor as yourself."
>
> Matthew 22:37–39

I had every excuse in the book for not loving my neighbor, and a few I'm sure God had never heard before—but I couldn't find an asterisk or exemption to get me off the hook. After months of arguing with God, I finally knocked on my neighbors' doors and invited them for coffee at my kitchen table.

When it was my neighbors' turn to knock on my door, most of them were as nervous as I was. We learned each other's names, we laughed and talked and shared, and these strangers walked out my door as friends. You'll meet some of them in these pages, although names have been changed to protect their privacy.

I invited my neighbors back for a Bible study, and we've been meeting regularly ever since! I kept notes on what worked well and what failed miserably, how my neighbors responded, and every mistake I made. A ministry called the Neighborhood Café was born, and I've been honored to share my experience with women across the United States and Canada—and even Australia!

I didn't want to be a freak or fanatic. I just wanted to be their friend.

Hosting a neighborhood Bible study might not be your cup of tea, but I bet you can't find an exception clause either. This book will give you tips, tools, and techniques you need to love your neighbor in your own unique way. You'll learn how to maximize your time by offering simple hospitality—not extravagant entertaining—to many neighbors at once. If that sounds about as much fun as a root canal, you'll also discover dozens of ideas to connect with your neighbors perfectly suited for different personalities. You'll be relieved to know there are natural ways to get to know your neighbors without being weird, and you'll overcome fears about sharing your faith and find fulfillment in obeying Christ's #2 command. You can make new friends with women who were once strangers as you form authentic relationships while creating a safe, secure community to live and raise your family.

I speak from the field: I have been there, done that—and lived to tell about it! There's no excuse I haven't had myself. There's no mistake I haven't made. I don't have enough time to do this either. I don't have all the answers. My house could always be cleaner.

Yet when our love for God overflows onto our neighbors, our communities become stronger, our streets are safer, and we'll even live longer. Most important, more people end up in heaven.

And as God's grace reaches more and more people, there will be great thanksgiving, and God will receive more and more glory.

2 Corinthians 4:15

In today's culture, it's weird to love your neighbor—but we don't have to be weird doing it. Thank you for being just the right kind of weird with me.

—Amy

# 1

# The View From My Window

The contemporary 1960s living room was a far cry from the Catholic cathedral where she attended mass as a child, but my newlywed mother couldn't refuse when her neighbor invited her to a Bible study in her home. Over coffee and cookies, they discussed a book together and memorized a Scripture my mother can still rattle off to this day. While the other women prayed, this shy, pretty girl with a beehive hairdo peeked out through her cat-eye glasses with diamonds on each corner and saw the other women talking to God as if He were real—as if He could really hear them and cared what they had to say.

My father, laid up at home with a broken leg, started reading the only thing he could reach without getting his crutches—my mother's book from Bible study, *The Kneeling Christian*. He read it from back to front, then from front to back. Then he knelt awkwardly on his one good leg and accepted Jesus Christ as his Savior.

Both my parents became Christians the year before I was born. By the time I came along, both my parents loved God with all their hearts. They loved my brother and me. Our family played and prayed together, ate home-cooked meals together, read the Bible together, and went to church together.

My favorite television show when I was a child was *Little House on the Prairie*. When Laura Ingalls bowed her braided pigtails and asked God to forgive her sins, I knelt with my daddy and prayed along with her. My mother, father, and I were baptized together at the same time—a triple dunk! I wrote this in my diary on January 10, 1979:

> JANUARY 10 — Happy Birthday to me! ♪♪♪
>
> Dear Diary,
> Nell,
> today is the big day. I've been a Christian for two years. 2 years ago today at 9:00 I sat down and asked the Lord to save my life. It feels so good to have been a Christian. In school we had art. We made snowman mobils. I think mine is real cute.

*Happy Birthday to me!*

*Dear Diary,*

*Well, today is the big day! I've been a Christian for two years. 2 years ago today at 9:00 I sat down and asked the*

*Lord to save my life. It feels so good to have been a Christian. In school we had art. We made snowman mobils [sic]. I think mine is real cute.*

Here's another excerpt from my diary at the age of nine—

*Dear Diary,*
*There's something I have to write about. Every night I cry myself to sleep. Every night I feel so bad about it. Every time my mom or dad asks me to do one of them a favor, I make a [sic] ugly face. Joe has been sick at least 5 times this month, and when he's sick he gets all of the attention. It makes me feel so left out or lonely. I've asked God to help me. I know I'm jealous of Joe, but I just can't help it. I told Mom and Dad how I felt, but they sort of ignored me. Things like that are what make me all sad. It makes me want to run away and cry. See ya.*

This is my earliest memory of God: He was my Helper when life got tough (and my brother got all the attention), my Confidant who listened to my woes, my Friend who knew me best. I promise, my parents were justified if they ignored my melodramatic whining!

My parents did almost everything right, but I still chose to do almost everything wrong. If I had managed to keep up with that diary for a few more years, it would have read something like this—

*Dear Diary,*
*I am tired of being called goody-two-shoes. I want to be popular. I want to be invited to parties. I want friends to pass me secret notes between classes. But most of all, I want a boyfriend. I want to be accepted and liked. I want to belong.*

In high school it didn't "feel so good" to be a Christian anymore. And so from the time I was fifteen until I was thirty-five, I walked away from God. I didn't lose my beliefs, but I lost my faith. I still *believed* the Bible stories I'd been taught, I still *believed* God loved me—I just didn't want anything to do with church or prayer or the actual live-like-you-believe-it stuff.

I was afraid to trust God and believe that His ways were better than the ways of the popular kids I wanted to impress. I was afraid of rejection. I was afraid of being picked on or singled out. I was afraid of being different. I was afraid of being lonely.

I gave in to my fears and my feelings, and walked away from my faith.

My wedding to that boyfriend I so desperately wanted was one of the last times I went to church for a long time, except for occasional holidays to pacify my parents. When they prayed at the start of the service, I prayed it would end! While they worshiped, I wondered what was for dinner. And as they sang all umpteen verses of "Just As I Am," I would harden my heart once again and say, "Just as I am is perfectly *fine*, thank you very much!"

> My parents did almost everything right, but I still chose to do almost everything wrong.

As an adult I avoided church, and I wasn't teaching our daughter my beliefs. My husband and I enrolled Emma at a local Christian school because we thought they offered the best academic curriculum—we were just going to keep an eye on all that "Jesus stuff." I knew many of the parents and staff from my churchgoing days, and they thought they knew me. I could sling their Christian lingo and stop cussing and smoking long enough to get through a parent-teacher meeting!

## Smoke 'Em If You Got 'Em

Except for the time I was pregnant and nursing, I smoked for the entire twenty years I was away from God. Is smoking a sin? I don't think so. But I wasn't being very smart, and I certainly wasn't being a good steward of God's creation. Smoking was crippling my body, and it was also crippling my confidence by making me feel unworthy and embarrassed. I hid my smoking from most people, so my habit limited my relationships as I worked my schedule around when and where I was going to sneak my next cigarette.

> I gave in to my fears and my feelings, and walked away from my faith.

I loved smoking; I really did. I enjoyed it; smoking was relaxing and pleasurable. My day was synchronized around my smoking—with my morning coffee, after lunch, in the car, before bed. What I didn't enjoy was constantly carrying gum, perfume, and hand sanitizer, being afraid of people stopping by my home unexpectedly, hiding my habit from people, wasting money—and most of all, I hated the example I was setting for my daughter. As she got older, she began to nag me about it. She was getting to be a real drag on my drag.

## My Good, Godly Girlfriends

Hanging out at the jungle gym while our kids played after school, the other parents would often ask, "Where do you go to church?" I would reply with a sideways glance, "Oh, we don't have a church home," as if we were pitiful, pious waifs on a desperate search for a house of worship to call our own. In reality, I religiously enjoyed my coffee, crossword puzzle, and cigarettes every Sunday morning.

21

When they found out we didn't go to church, can you believe not one single person invited me to go to church with her?

Instead, they invited me out for coffee. We worked together on committees and school carnivals. Our children played at each other's homes.

I saw firsthand how these women relied on God to make them good mommies even when their kids behaved badly. I saw how they responded when they didn't agree with each other. I overheard their heartfelt prayers and realized their beliefs went beyond simple Bible stories.

> As we became friends very naturally, I began to soften spiritually.

Like my own sweet momma peeking during prayer, I saw that what they had was real, and their relationship with God made a difference in the way they lived. They had hope and joy even as they took children to chemotherapy and buried beloved parents. They were content planning fundraisers instead of exotic vacations.

They were simply lovely, and they simply loved me.

As we became friends very naturally, I began to soften spiritually. One day I realized I truly wanted to be the person I was pretending to be around them.

Smoking—one of the harbingers of my rebellion—was also one of the first signs of my renewal. I'll never forget when I made the decision to quit. Walking through the school to pick Emma up from class, I envisioned myself with the cigarette I had just thrown out the window still dangling from my hand (go ahead and add littering to my list of offenses). I thought, *If these people could see me as I really was, I would be mortified and they would be terrified.* Later, I realized this was the Holy Spirit whispering to my soul, revealing a thirst for righteousness I would never have (nor could have) admitted.

I had seen a poster that suggested setting a quit date would be helpful, so I set a date a few weeks out and told a few people (including my daughter!) I was going to quit smoking on October 15. The accountability was nerve-wracking, but it helped me prepare mentally. I didn't want to go from one chemical dependency to another, so I didn't use the patch or gum—I just quit cold turkey . . . and mashed potatoes, with extra gravy, and a candy bar for dessert. Controlling my eating when I quit smoking was very difficult because I craved that hand-to-mouth movement after a meal. Instead of having an after-dinner cigarette, I had an after-dinner *dinner* and just kept eating. The actual average weight gain from quitting smoking is only about five pounds, but I blew that theory out of the water. Later—too late for me!—I read that you should drink a glass of water to satisfy cravings. So, there you have my tips to quit smoking: set a quit date, tell some people, and drink lots of water. Now I'd add lots and lots of prayer—prayers of thanksgiving and prayers for mercy!

I wondered if God would be angry, irritated, or annoyed with me after so many years of ignoring Him. But as I tilted my head ever so slightly toward the Lord's voice and let one little corner of my heart soften toward Him, I swear I heard Him say, "Oh, Amy—I love you! I've been waiting for you, and I'm so happy you're back!"

> I swear I heard Him say, "Oh, Amy—I love you! I've been waiting for you, and I'm so happy you're back!"

As Romans 2:4 says, God was so "wonderfully kind, tolerant and patient" with me. No one lectured me back to church. It wasn't a condemning pamphlet or a churchy program that softened my heart. Instead, God's kindness in sending Jesus Christ as my Savior—and His kindness revealed through the people He placed around me—turned me from my sin. God didn't demand that I clean up my act before I came to Him—but He kindly, gently, and sweetly revealed areas where I was making my own rules, then He gave me the desire, wisdom, and strength to submit to Him.

Please take it from this former pagan turned passionate follower—we need each other! We all need someone like Adelle and Donna, Julie and Margaret, Michelle and Marilyn, Luann and Lane—the women whose lives led me back toward the Lord. I call them my good, godly girlfriends—or my gGg's for short.

Natural relationships changed my spiritual destiny. This is why I'm passionate about helping us connect with each other. We need more than an hour of church on Sunday. We need friends around us all day, every day—in the trenches of our living rooms and the battleground of the playground. We need fearless women who are brave enough to tell us when we're wrong and wise enough to remind us of God's righteousness.

> We need fearless women who are brave enough to tell us when we're wrong and wise enough to remind us of God's righteousness.

We need friends who will not always take our side but will always take our hand. They will walk with us side-by-side through the mud and muck of life's messes and sing praises with us when God straightens things out. They'll gently point out when we're out of line, and offer God's Word as the only way out. They let us moan and complain, but they know when enough is enough. You won't hear their advice on daytime pop psychology shows; they aren't afraid to defy Dr. Phil. Little did I know, but I would need their counsel soon.

## Revival Is Reviled

When God used these natural relationships to steer me spiritually, I started going to church and reading my Bible, and I attended several different Bible studies at any church that cracked its doors open. With my smoking behind me, I could spend so much time with other women. It was a joy! But at home . . . not so much. While this was an exciting time of renewal in my relationship with God, it was a time of incredible stress in my relationship with my husband—I mean, this changed *everything*!

If you had peeped inside our picture window, you would have seen a very frustrated wife and a hurting husband in the middle of

> Revival is reviled in Satan's kingdom. It will always come under attack.

a terrifying spiritual battle. I cried out to God, "Seriously? This is what I get? I thought following you was supposed to make everything *better*!"

But it wasn't better. Everything was worse. Our "typical" married fights over money, sex, and parenting were replaced with screaming-at-the-top-of-our-lungs arguments about television evangelists, Bible translations, and how much time I spent at church.

It took many sleepless nights and early morning soul-searching sessions before I realized what was happening: The stakes were too high for the devil to leave us alone. Revival is reviled in Satan's kingdom. It will always come under attack, and the devil is a ruthless enemy—he attacks us spiritually, relationally, emotionally, financially, and physically.

We almost didn't make it . . . *almost*! But God redeemed so many mistakes I made in the way I responded and reacted to my husband. He exchanged our broken, bruised, fragile marriage for a stronger relationship with Christ at the center. Tougher times lay ahead—in fact, each new phase of my personal faith and ministry has been accompanied by bitter fights, relational trauma, and hurt feelings. I don't think I'll ever get used to it, and I'm rarely thankful *for* it . . . but now I'm thankful *through* these challenges, and I trust God to reign and restore.

We triumphed in round one against Satan's minions, and together we enrolled in ministry school. I soaked up God's Word and fell in love with my first love all over again—and my second love, too.

## "She Speaks"—Maybe . . .

One wintry morning as we neared the end of ministry school, loyal dog at my feet and hot coffee in my hand, I sat in my usual spot on my yellow loveseat by my picture window with my Bible and journal and wrote, "I'd like to share what I'm learning with other people." The journal was soon filled with dozens of different ideas, topics, and verses the Lord and I explored together . . . but I had no idea what to do with this list! Maybe, I thought, I was going to have a very holy dog—she was the only one who ever heard these revelations!

At the top of the page, I wrote a website address for a women's ministry conference called She Speaks. Their website said it was for "women who share a passion to step out with the messages God has placed on our hearts." I assumed they would step out to *people*, not just pets, so I registered—only to find it was sold out. I was number 250 on the waiting list for a conference that only held 650 people—but God moved a few mountains and I was able to attend![1]

In the days before GPS, my printed Google map directed me to the middle of a North Carolina cornfield. By the time I arrived I was hurried and harried and having a bad hair day. Finally—after months of planning and hours of driving—I took my seat, took a deep breath, took a look around . . . and burst into tears. What was I doing here? I was alone. I was outclassed. I was underqualified. I was unworthy. It was a waste of money for me to come here. I was in way over my head!

But it was at that conference that one of the speakers uttered three little words that made my heart race—and as soon as I heard her say "neighborhood Bible study," I knew what I was going to do with that list. For the first time, I could see how God had aligned my revival, my training, my trials, and my passion. I was following hard after Him, I was devouring His Word, I had a heart of compassion toward others, and I was busting to share all He had done in my home.

I returned home from the conference with a plan to invite my neighbors over for coffee and cookies, then lure them back for Bible study! It was going to be called The Rosewood Café because we lived on Rosewood Drive. I opened my journal and drew a little logo, jotted down what I would say on the invitation, and even set the date. There was only one little problem with my plan to start a neighborhood Bible study: I did not know my neighbors.

> There was only one little problem: I did not know my neighbors.

## Won't You Be My Neighbor?

My husband and I lived in four houses in three states in two years. One of the neighborhoods where we lived was filled with families who had been there for many years—everybody knew everybody else, and quite a bit of their business, too. You couldn't take a walk without someone stopping to ask about your mother or your leaky basement. Another neighborhood was filled with the sounds of children playing while neighbors chatted in the cul-de-sac. You didn't dare run out to the mailbox without makeup because you were sure to run into a kindly neighbor who would offer to get your groceries while she was out. Another neighborhood was brand-new—no one knew anyone, and everyone walked around shell-shocked as they sorted out this unfamiliar place.

> I hadn't even **known** my neighbors in some of the places I had lived, let alone **loved** them.

After all that moving around, we finally landed in a home less than one mile from where we started. Our new neighborhood was quiet and peaceful . . . so eerily quiet, in fact, that you could take a long walk on a beautiful Sunday afternoon and not see a single soul. I had been looking out my picture window for over seven years on the corner of Rosewood and Longwood Drives, yet I knew only a handful of my neighbors. I recognized their cars and their dogs, but not their faces. I didn't know their joys or their pains, I had no one to call to borrow a cup of sugar, and I had never told them about Jesus. He was trapped in my house . . . and I wasn't sure I was ready to let Him out!

I felt guilty about Christ's command to love my neighbors:

> "You must love the Lord your God with all your heart, all your soul, and all your mind." This is the first and greatest commandment. A second is equally important: "Love your neighbor as yourself."
>
> Matthew 22:37–39

This command is reinforced in the New Testament books of Mark, Luke, Romans, Galatians, and James—and they're just quoting the Old Testament book of Leviticus.[2] I hadn't even *known* my neighbors in some of the places I had lived, let alone *loved* them.

## Don't Be Weird

I blazed a twenty-year trail where God never intended me to tread, following my own rules and ignoring Him. He welcomed me back with open arms, healed my hurts, helped me conquer habits and hang-ups, and gave me godly girlfriends. Yet when it came time to return the favor—no, that's impossible, let me say it another way—when it came time to express the fullness of my love for Him by loving my neighbor, I balked.

I was not ready to be "that girl." I did not want to be weird. I was less concerned about trusting God and more concerned with impressing my neighbors. I was afraid of rejection. I was afraid of being picked on or singled out. I was afraid of being different. I was afraid of being left out and lonely. Sound familiar? I was haunted by the same fears that had followed me all my life. The difference is that when I had these fears as a teen, I went out and mingled with the wrong crowd. As an adult, I kept myself cloistered in Bible studies and church activities—all in the name of holiness. But really, it was fear.

> I was not ready to be "that girl." I did not want to be weird.

My fears emboldened me to argue with God. I asked Him, "*Who* is my neighbor? Don't you count it as 'loving my neighbor' when I support a child in Ethiopia with a donation every month? Isn't it 'loving my neighbor' when I give to my church and they help missionaries all over the world? By 'neighbor,' you mean everyone in the whole wide world, don't you?"

I questioned *how* to love my neighbor. "You didn't really explain exactly what you mean by 'love your neighbor as yourself.' Do you expect me to spend every weekend grilling out together? Do you want me to walk them down the Roman Road every time they walk down my sidewalk? Can't I just slap a fish bumper sticker on my minivan, wear Jesus jewelry to the grocery store, and put out yard signs for my church's Easter cantata?"

I cheered for the lawyer who cross-examined Jesus in Luke 10. Oh, he understood Command #1 (love God) and Command #2 (love your neighbor) all right . . . but he wanted to make himself look good. Jesus replied with the parable of the Good Samaritan. You may have heard it—

Jesus replied with a story: "A Jewish man was traveling from Jerusalem down to Jericho, and he was attacked by bandits. They stripped him of his clothes, beat him up, and left him half dead beside the road.

"By chance a priest came along. But when he saw the man lying there, he crossed to the other side of the road and passed him by. A Temple assistant walked over and looked at him lying there, but he also passed by on the other side.

"Then a despised Samaritan came along, and when he saw the man, he felt compassion for him. Going over to him, the Samaritan soothed his wounds with olive oil and wine and bandaged them. Then he put the man on his own donkey and took him to an inn, where he took care of him. The next day he handed the innkeeper two silver coins, telling him, 'Take care of this man. If his bill runs higher than this, I'll pay you the next time I'm here.'

"Now which of these three would you say was a neighbor to the man who was attacked by bandits?" Jesus asked.

The man replied, "The one who showed him mercy."

Then Jesus said, "Yes, now go and do the same."

Luke 10:30–37

Jesus blew up my definition of *neighbor* with this parable. The Jews defined the Greek word *plēsion* (play-SEE-on) as neighbor or friend, but they lived in tight-knit communities with only their fellow Hebrews. To the Jews, "love your neighbor *as yourself*" meant "love your neighbor *who is just like you*." I only knew a few of my neighbors, and—permission to speak honestly, please?—some of them were a little annoying. Surely loving my neighbor didn't include the ones with barking dogs and loud parties! I related to the Jews on this one: I wanted to love my neighbors whose houses looked like mine, whose families acted like mine, the ones who carried little doggie litter bags when they walked in front of my house. It's easy to love *those* neighbors!

These two men could not have been more different. Had he not been a beaten, bloodied, and bruised mess, the Jewish man likely would have spit in the face of the Samaritan who helped him. Jews hated Samaritans; they considered them unclean and uncouth. Yet Jesus united these two mortal enemies through a crisis, compassion, and caregiving. The Samaritan was moved to action. He used his own resources to soothe and bandage his new friend. He walked the dusty road while holding the Jewish man steady on his own donkey. He spent the night by his side, tending his wounds, soothing his cries. He invested time and money and made a commitment to a long-term relationship. He showed mercy—the Greek word is *eleos* (ELL-ee-oss), "kindness or good will towards the miserable and the afflicted, joined with a desire to help them."[3]

Jesus defined *neighbor* as anyone and everyone—regardless of their nationality or religion—with whom we live or whom we have the chance to meet. The Vulgate, a Latin translation of the Bible, uses the word *proximus* for neighbor. It means

> I wanted to love my neighbors whose houses looked like mine, whose families acted like mine, the ones who carried little doggie litter bags when they walked in front of my house. It's easy to love **those** neighbors!

"the nearest person or thing." It shares the same root as *proximity* and *approximate*. I, on the other hand, had globalized the definition of *neighbor* to include everyone in the whole wide world, conveniently excluding the people who live right next door.

Did Jesus want me to love the women in *my* neighborhood, the ones who could reject me? Right to my face?

I would rather go to Africa than go across the street.

After months of debate (read: disobedience) about this crazy neighborhood Bible study idea, I invited my neighbors over for coffee. At first, I was afraid and intimidated. It felt awkward. It wasn't always easy. But now? Since I've met Juanita and Linda, Mary Ann and Mary Sharon, Bonnie and Lauren? And since my neighbors sat together in my living room last night and talked and laughed and cried and prayed?

Oh, yeah—the reward was worth the risk.

In the years since that first coffee klatch, I've knocked on my neighbors' doors hundreds of times. Every time I invite my neighbors over for coffee, I make a new mistake. Sometimes I wait too long to send the invitation, sometimes I send it too early. I forget my neighbors' names. I don't have enough food, or I get so distracted that I don't enjoy my guests. I forget to follow up with a hurting friend, or I'm lax to thank someone for coming.

> I would rather go to Africa than go across the street.

Every time I engage with my neighbors, I learn something new. This book is a candid compilation of my own mistakes while giving glory to God for any success. It's also the story of others across the country who have marched down their sidewalks, raised quivering hands to knock on their neighbors' doors, and returned home with the names of new friends.

And that's how we roll on Rosewood Drive.

## Five Minutes of Obedience

People who know me today are surprised by my stories—"I can't believe you smoked!" they exclaim when they meet me at my job in a church. When they hear me speak about friendships that now dot my neighborhood, they say, "I can't believe you didn't know your neighbors!" And my personal favorite, "I can't believe you fight with your husband!"

I had no idea that quitting smoking was the start of my journey back to God. The first time I cracked open my dusty Bible, I had no idea its words would transform my life. When I sat myself down in a pew and it wasn't Christmas or Easter, I had no idea I would eventually be on staff at a church. The first time my husband and I held hands to pray together, I had no idea these prayers could literally hold us together. All I knew was that these were the next best steps I needed to take personally. I had no idea that inviting Jesus into my life would impact my marriage and my daughter and my neighborhood and my church—and eventually people all over the country would hear about Christ's incredible mercy on me. No idea! If I did, I probably would have been scared to death. But it happened very gradually, very naturally. It wasn't weird.

God has an irritating habit of pulling me out of my comfort zone and into His Kingdom come. Is there something today that God has asked you to do, some little step of obedience that you are resisting or struggling against? I struggled too! Maybe He's nudging you to stop an unhealthy habit or start something new. Maybe He's challenging you to take a class, start a conversation, make amends, or memorize a verse. I know He's already asked you to love your neighbor.

I encourage you to take that terrifying first step.

You may look back in nine days or nine months or nine years and say, "Wow! I can't believe *this* is what God had in store for me!" His plan for your life and for your personal ministry in your home, on your street, at your job, or in your church doesn't unfold all at once. Each morning the sun comes up gradually, each sunset fades slowly, each step is taken incrementally one at a time. Oswald Chambers said, "If you obey God in the first thing He shows you, then He instantly opens up the next truth to you. You could read volumes on the work of the Holy Spirit, when five minutes of total, uncompromising obedience would make things as clear as sunlight."[4]

You can trust God to hold your hand as you take your next best steps. You can trust that His plan is good. His way can be tough. It is not the path of least resistance . . . but it is the path of best results!

Your neighbors are in crisis. They are by the side of the road—your road, in your neighborhood. Will you walk on by? Or will you be moved with compassion? Will you stop? Will you care?

## Next Best Steps

1. Have you ever pretended to be someone you're not? When we get tired of our charade, there are three options: blow your cover, bow out, or become who you're pretending to be. Which did you do?

2. Who are your gGg's? Plan a special time to get together so you can tell them how much they've meant to you, or send a handwritten card of appreciation. If you don't have a good, godly girlfriend, ask God to bring someone special into your life.

3. Have you ever experienced a setback just as you were stepping into a new phase of your faith? How did you get through this trying time? Who helped you? Did your faith become stronger or was it undermined? When it happens again, how will you respond?

4. What is the view from your window? Describe the relationships you have in your neighborhood. Do you know your neighbors? Have you ever had a spiritual conversation with a neighbor?

5. Where is God asking you for "five minutes of total, uncompromising obedience"? Have you been arguing and debating with Him about anything He is nudging you to do? Recall a time you obeyed God first and asked questions later. How does obedience make things clear?

# Welcome to Your Neighborhood

My neighbor's purple and blue Christmas lights are quite festive. She's an artist—a bona fide artiste who teaches art at a local museum; her works are displayed at art festivals and in galleries. The hallway to her basement studio is lined with hand-painted frescoes and her rooms are filled with her own stunning mixed-media artwork. Her window blinds adjust from the top or the bottom, and they are always arranged in interesting, asymmetrical patterns. And each Christmas, she artistically strings a tree in their yard with a single strand of blue lights and a single strand of purple lights.

Did you catch that? "My neighbor's *blue* and *purple* Christmas lights . . ." It just doesn't sound right, does it? If I didn't know Tori was an artist, I might be annoyed with her off-color decorating and crooked blinds. But since I've seen the creative abilities God has given her, I appreciate her talent and unique perspective.

Another home in my neighborhood is very contemporary, with peaked glass windows and modern architecture—but inside I was surprised to find it was full of antiques! The sweet homeowner served me tea, proudly showed me her treasures, and shared stories about her travels. Corrine wistfully told me, "I'm new around here. I hardly know anyone." When I asked how long she'd lived here, she answered, "Fifteen years." Since meeting Corrine, not only do I appreciate her sense of style, but I vow that no one will live in my neighborhood for fifteen years without meeting a friend!

For years I made assumptions about the people living inside the homes in my neighborhood based on what I saw outside. I assumed they were comfy and cozy based on their tidy lawns and neat hedges. I assumed they were irresponsible and uncaring based on their barking dogs or weedy sidewalks. I assumed they were sacrilegious and unsaved based on the cars in their driveways on Sunday mornings.

> We judge books by their covers; we judge neighbors by their cars and houses.

One-fifth of Americans admit they judge their neighbors based on the condition and appearance of their homes or property, but I'm willing to bet this number is much higher. We judge books by their covers; we judge neighbors by their cars and houses. According to the Pew Internet and American Life Project, 28 percent of us do not know *any* of our neighbors by name![1] Yet we assume we know all about them.

Do you know your neighbors' names? If you're a suburban baby boomer–homeowner in the Midwest, chances are you know more of your neighbors' names than a hipster urban Millennial from the West Coast would.

- Homeowners are more likely than renters to know their neighbors' names (61 percent versus 39 percent).
- Midwesterners are more likely to be able to say hello by name (60 percent) than those living in the Northeast (51 percent), South (51 percent), or western states (49 percent).
- Suburbanites living in single-family homes know more of their neighbors' names (54 percent) than urbanites living in apartments, attached townhouses, or other multi-unit buildings (46 percent).
- Sixty-three percent of your neighbors over age fifty-five know your name, while only about 52 percent of your middle-aged neighbors age thirty-five to fifty-five can greet you by name—but 60 percent of your eighteen- to thirty-four-year-old neighbors have absolutely no idea who you are.[2]

## Where Everybody Knows Your Name

Jesus commanded us to love our neighbors with the same urgency and intensity as we love God—

> "You must love the Lord your God with all your heart, all your soul, and all your mind." This is the first and greatest commandment. A second is equally important: "Love your neighbor as yourself."
>
> Matthew 22:37–39

The Jews (and maybe I) wanted to love their neighbors who were *the same as* themselves. The little Greek adverb for "as" is *hōs*. It's used in comparisons—*as, like as, even as, in the same manner as*—so it connects two words and makes them equal. Love your neighbor as yourself. Your neighbor and yourself. Equal in the eyes of God, equally loved and known by God.

Jesus knew each of His disciples by name. Andrew, Bartholomew, James (times two), John, Judas, Jude, Matthew, Peter, Philip, Simon, and Thomas—He knew their names, their nicknames, their families, where they grew up, their personalities. I wonder if He affectionately spoke their names and recalled a special memory with each of them as He washed their feet at the Last Supper the day before He was crucified. Even Judas would run to betray Him on freshly washed feet. Jesus told them, "I have given you an example to follow. Do *as* I have done to you" (John 13:15, emphasis added).

> It's pretty hard to love someone when you don't even know their name.

In a way that only Jesus can, He upped the ante on the #2 command. Jesus said we should love our neighbors *as, like as, even as, in the same manner as* He has loved us. Later that same evening, He also said, "This is my commandment: Love each other *in the same way* I have loved you" (John 15:12, emphasis added).

The thing is, it's pretty hard to love someone when you don't even know their name.

You know your own name and the stories behind the nicknames your friends and family call you. You know the nights you've cried yourself to sleep and the mornings you've woken with praise on your lips. You know when you've needed a friend or a garden hoe or a teaspoon of some strange spice but you don't want to buy a whole bottle. You know you're good at photography but you can't sew on a button; you can write a thank-you card but not a speech; you can kill a plastic houseplant but your goldfish live forever. You know your needs, your wants, your dreams, your fears, your strengths, your weaknesses, and your abilities.

Do you know as much about your neighbors? Do you know what keeps them awake at night? Do you know their struggles or their joys? Do you know their stories, their history, their dreams for the future? Do you know they have a full bottle of turmeric you can use for your chili recipe, and they would love you to take a picture of their prize rose before it wilts? Do you know if they know Jesus? How will you know their hearts' desires if you don't even know their names?

Peter, who begged Jesus to wash his hands and head not just his feet, would later write, "For God called you to do good, even if it means suffering, *just as* Christ suffered for you. He is your example, and you must follow in his steps" (1 Peter 2:21, emphasis added).

There is no biblical command given to us that Christ has not already obeyed and demonstrated! He showed us how He loved His neighbors, and we can follow His footsteps right into our own neighborhoods.

## Who Is Your Neighbor?

"Birds of a feather flock together" isn't a biblical directive, but it is a proven demographic fact. Your neighbors—those who choose to live in the same neighborhood as you—may reflect your same education, income, family status, hobbies, interests, taste, and values even more than your extended family.

Whether you live in a downtown condo or on a country ranch, on a tree-lined lane or a gang-infested street, I know this fact about your neighborhood: Inside every home are people hungry for personal attention, meaningful relationships, and real friendships. You are surrounded by young singles and new parents, families raising teenagers while caring for elderly parents, empty-nesters, and elderly widows. Some are executives; others are homemakers. They are sick and well, happy and sad, churched and unchurched. You might live right down the street from some of these ladies:

- **Religious Rita:** attends church regularly and never misses a noodle dinner
- **Pagan Patty:** sunbathes on Sunday yet never darkens the church door
- **Faithful Felicity:** prays for the opportunity to meet other women but doesn't know how
- **Unsaved Sue:** doesn't even know what she doesn't know
- **Wondering Wendy:** dabbles in the God-thing but has no one to answer her questions
- **Athletic Ann:** finds her self-worth in her workouts
- **Widowed Wilma:** is overwhelmed with solitude
- **Single-Parent Pam:** does double duty as both Mom and Dad
- **Executive Alexis:** brings home the bacon and sometimes manages to fry it up in a pan
- **Stay-at-Home-Mom Molly:** wonders if she'll ever have a conversation that doesn't involve the potty
- **Busybody Betty:** knows the scoop and loves to dish it out
- **Saintly Sally:** has a godly legacy she's eager to share

The good news is, the majority of these neighbors already like you—and if they know your name, they like you even more (66 percent compared to 80 percent). Only 5 percent of Americans don't like the people who live around them, but if you run over their peonies or play your music too loud, they're more likely to ignore you (31 percent) than to start an argument (4 percent).[3]

> God may be calling you to say, think, or do something today that will impact your neighbors' lives for eternity.

What else do all your neighbors have in common? They all live near you, a Christian who is commanded to love them. What

41

do they all need? To know Jesus Christ. God may be calling you to say, think, or do something today that will impact your neighbors' lives for eternity. You can create a community of friends—people of all faiths or no faith, from all churches or no church, of all ages, at all stages of life—who draw on each other as they draw near to Christ.

## Discouraged Disciples

If you ran into me in the grocery store and I was wearing my half-marathon finisher's jacket, you would silently ask yourself, *Hmmm . . . wonder who she borrowed that from?*

I don't look like a runner (especially when I run). Nevertheless, in 2012, I ran, jogged, walked, limped, crawled, and cried my way across 13.1 miles of pavement. This was preceded by weeks of setting my alarm for 4:30 a.m. to train on hills and run a medieval torture method called fartleks (yes, that is spelled correctly).

A lot of that training was done in my neighborhood. As I ran past my neighbors' homes, I wondered what was happening behind their closed doors—

*I used to see them working in their yard every weekend, but I heard he had an affair. . . . I haven't seen her much since her granddaughter came to live with her. I wonder if her son is out of jail yet. . . . That yard sure needs a mow! She's a single mom, it must be hard. . . . I should stop and see her. We haven't visited since her husband's funeral. . . .*

For many of my neighbors, life isn't turning out as they planned. They may feel like the disciples in Luke 24. Days before in Jerusalem, these two men had just seen their hope crucified and their community torn apart. They, too, wondered about life's disappointments as they traveled the road between Jerusalem and their hometown, a place called Emmaus, a seven-mile journey.

The road to Emmaus is just like Rosewood Drive, or Main Street, or James Road. It's the intersection of the formal place of worship and the place where we really need Jesus—right in our own homes. It's where the serenity of the sanctuary meets the screaming baby and ringing doorbell. It's what Romans 12:1 calls "your everyday, ordinary life—your sleeping, eating, going-to-work, and walking-around life" (THE MESSAGE).

Look how Jesus enters the story: "As they talked and discussed these things, Jesus himself suddenly came and began walking with them" (Luke 24:15).

Jesus casually started a conversation, like you might do while waiting in line at the grocery store or playing at the neighborhood park. The root of the phrase translated "came" means "the curve or inner angle of the arm, the bent arm." Picture Jesus putting His arm around their shoulders as He got in step and started walking along with them. They didn't even know it was Jesus; they could not recognize Him, yet they were comfortable—He was easy to talk to.

The next thing Jesus did was ask simple questions about what was happening in their lives right then: "He asked them, 'What are you discussing so intently as you walk along?'" (Luke 24:17).

Isn't Jesus brilliant? He didn't dazzle them with theology or lecture them about their ignorance. He simply cared about what was on their minds at that very moment.

These men thought they knew what went down in Jerusalem that weekend. They explained,

> [Jesus] was a prophet who did powerful miracles, and he was a mighty teacher in the eyes of God and all the people. But our leading priests and other religious leaders handed him over to be condemned to death, and they crucified him. We had hoped he was the Messiah who had come to rescue Israel.
>
> Luke 24:19–21

Just like the men on the road to Emmaus, most of our neighbors know part of the Gospel: "Jesus was a great man. He was crucified. He died. Some people said He rose again." Sadly, most people get no farther, and, as a result, they fight the same discouragement as the disciples did . . .

*Religion isn't all it's cracked up to be. I tried church, but it didn't do me any good. I prayed a whole bunch of prayers. God didn't answer any of them. I still lost my job. My kids still hate me. I don't know what's the big deal with all that Jesus stuff. I had hoped it would help me, but it didn't.*

> Just like the men on the road to Emmaus, most of our neighbors know part of the Gospel.

This is the heartsick cry of a woman who hasn't met Jesus on the road home from church.

## A Common Meal

Jesus went into the disciples' home in Emmaus and sat down with them at the kitchen table. The children hurried to put away their toys and wash their faces. The wives reached for an extra bowl. Each of them spooned a little less soup to leave enough for their unexpected guest.

This meal did not rank among the miraculous meals, like the feeding of the thousands. It wasn't a sacramental meal, like the Last Supper. This was a common, ordinary, everyday meal—at the table, in the house. Jesus took their loaf of bread and blessed it. Perhaps He prayed along the lines of this traditional Jewish prayer: "Blessed are you, Lord our God, King of the Universe, who brings forth bread from the earth." As the Bread of Life, brought forth from an earthen grave, blessed their common meal, God opened the disciples' eyes so that they recognized Him as their risen Lord.

Do you see Jesus in the common, everyday moments of your life? He is there as you make dinner and do laundry. He is there as you weed the flower bed and get the mail. He is there as you cry, and He is there as you laugh so hard that you make that embarrassing snort your kids tease you about.

The disciples didn't recognize Jesus until they shared this common meal. Then, when they finally recognized Him—POOF!—He disappeared.

Have you ever felt like—POOF!—Jesus disappeared?

Have you ever looked through the lingering smoke of this magic trick and wondered, *Lord, where did you go? I thought you were blessing my marriage, but we're fighting again. I thought you helped me get this job, but my new boss is a jerk. I thought my son had stopped doing drugs, but now he's in trouble again. Where did you go?*

I've often wondered why Jesus left the disciples just as their eyes were opened. Why were their eyes closed in the first place? Puritan Bible commentator Matthew Henry said Christ wanted to show them that He could teach them "by others, who should have His spiritual presence with them."[4] By hiding His identity, Christ demonstrated that the influence and impact of His Word didn't depend upon His physical presence.

> Do you see Jesus in the common, everyday moments of your life? He is there as you make dinner and do laundry. He is there as you weed the flower bed and get the mail.

He's left it up to us to be His body while He's not here. Girlfriends, we represent Jesus until He comes again! Does this terrify you as it does me?

Just when I'm not sure I can measure up, the Holy Spirit whispers, "I'm right here. Trust me." When Jesus has disappeared from your neighbor's view, He will use you to help her find Him again. He will use your arms to strengthen her. He will use your words to calm her. He will use your home to comfort her.

You live on the road to Emmaus, at the intersection of real life and religion.

## Take a Peek

What would we see if we could peek inside our typical American neighbor's home? On an average day, your neighbors spend:

- 8 hours and 44 minutes sleeping
- 48 minutes showering, dressing, and putting on makeup
- 7 hours and 33 minutes working, for the 41 percent of our neighbors who work
- 74 minutes eating
- 5 hours and 15 minutes for leisure and sports
- 18 minutes exercising[5]

Women do more work around the house, but they also get 40 more minutes of me-time each day.[6] The vast majority of their leisure time will be spent online on their computer, tablet, or smartphone. Most households are online, regardless of age—six out of ten of your senior neighbors over age 65 are online.[7] They do a little shopping, watch cute kitten videos, and connect with "friends" on social networks like Facebook.

I'm one of a growing number of Facebook fans. Using a conservative growth estimate, Facebook will have more users than China has residents by 2016.[8]

(Please excuse me while I go check Facebook.)

(Okay, I'm back.)

I just read that my friend Jodi is leaving on vacation (which I "liked"), Kelsey's having a birthday (I wrote a greeting on her Wall), and Michelle just finished a run (which secretly made me jealous, but I commented "woo hoo!" anyway). I often use Facebook Messenger to pray with people. No, there's nothing wrong with Facebook—but the world's largest social network fulfills only a tiny sliver of our social needs.

Forty percent of your neighbors spend more time socializing electronically than they do face-to-face (and 20 percent of them actually prefer it that way!).[9] From Millennials to baby boomers, your neighbors aged eighteen to sixty-four who use social networks check their Walls, post witty tweets, inform the world they are out of milk, upload selfies, and click the "like" button for 3.2 hours per day. When you factor in your neighbors who are

> **2 hours a day
> x 365 days a year
> = 30 total days a
> year with our faces
> buried in a screen.**

online but don't use social network websites, the average time on social networks drops to "only" two hours per day.[10] Seriously? Do the math: 2 hours a day x 365 days a year = 30 total days a year with our faces buried in a screen. What wouldn't you give to have a month with your girlfriends—at the beach, in a coffee shop, on your sofa? How would our relationships be different if we looked into each other's eyes for 730 hours per year?

Half of your young neighbors aged eighteen to thirty-four reach for Facebook as soon as their feet hit the floor every morning— more than a quarter of them check it out before they get out of bed.[11] Millennials are engaged in media for 17.8 hours per day. Half of this time is spent surfing the web, checking social media, and texting or chatting with friends; the other half is divided between watching television, playing computer games, watching movies, listening to the radio, and reading print magazines or newspapers. Obviously some of the media time overlaps, like when they watch television while checking Twitter and texting with friends. (I know a few teenagers who check Instagram in their sleep.) Thirty percent of the media content they consume is created by their peers, aka friends, followers, or fans.[12]

## An Epidemic of Loneliness

Despite having an average of 338 friends on Facebook,[13] the women in your neighborhood are plagued by what doctors and nurses have diagnosed as an epidemic of loneliness. Researchers say it's the quality of our social interaction, not the quantity, that best foretells loneliness, a condition that is literally killing us. Lonely people are more likely to be obese and experience memory loss, dementia, inflammation, depression, sleep disorders, and heart conditions. Lonely people are less likely to exercise or survive surgery. Loneliness increases levels of stress hormones. It impacts how long we live and how often we are sick.[14]

> 35 percent of all adults over forty-five are chronically lonely—a 75 percent increase in ten years.

In 1949, Hank Williams Senior wrote a song called "I'm So Lonesome I Could Cry." As a child, I listened to my dad's scratchy 45 over and over on my Raggedy Ann record player and painstakingly wrote the lyrics in my little diary. When this song first hit the airwaves, less than 10 percent of homes contained only one person. By 2010, this number had increased 250 percent. Today, one in four of the homes on your street is occupied by a single dweller.[15]

Living alone doesn't automatically make you lonely. You can feel lonely lying in bed with your husband in a house full of children; you can feel lonely in the middle of a party. You can be a loyal woman of faith and still feel lonely, because as we're transformed into the image of God we crave the relationships He designed us to enjoy.

Twenty-five percent of people say they have no one with whom they can discuss important matters. Another 20 percent said they have one—*one!*—good friend. A 2010 AARP study found that 35 percent of all adults over forty-five are chronically lonely—a 75 percent increase in ten years. And about 60 million people—20 percent of all Americans—are unhappy with their lives because of loneliness.[16]

Your neighbor may have 338 Facebook friends, but the average human is capable of intimately knowing only about 150 people.[17] Those extra 188 people filling up her feed are actually making her feel more lonely, not less! Research shows that passive scrolling of social media with the occasional "like" or comment increases feelings of loneliness. Maybe it's because no one tells the truth, the whole truth, and nothing but the truth on Facebook. No one brags about their pending bankruptcy or posts a selfie on a bad hair day, so it's easy to assume everyone is having more fun than we are or doing better than we are. Only when users actively participate in online conversations by making comments that take time and effort will they experience a decrease in loneliness and an improvement in relationships.[18]

> Social networks are a symptom of our need for relationships; they are not the solution.

Today, we tweet instead of talk; we communicate in code using our thumbs. We try to be "friends" without being friendly. Online interactions are no substitute for real-life conversations. Social networks are a *symptom* of our need for relationships; they are not the *solution*.

The solution is found smack dab in the middle of your neighborhood—the original social network—a convenient, comfortable, and non-threatening place to move from virtual friendships to real relationships. What would happen if we used our knuckles instead of our thumbs to communicate by knocking on our neighbors' doors?

## Use Virtual Technology to Make Real Friends

Are you Facebook friends with any of your neighbors? Capitalize on that technology and use it to obey Command #2. Do some creeping. Check out their pictures, read their last month of posts. Do they share apple pie recipes or political propaganda? Do they post about their grandchildren's antics or their aches and pains? What are their hobbies, what do they "like"? Use these insights to pray for your neighbors, and you'll be ready for a real conversation when God enables a real-life encounter.

You can create a private Facebook group for your neighborhood, where only approved members can see posts, or join NextDoor (www.nextdoor.com), a free private social network just for neighborhoods. In my neighborhood, we've used these networks to identify lost dogs and share coyote sightings; we've also planned a community yard sale, a block party, and a baby shower.

> Technology makes it easy to connect online, but our goal is to connect in real life.

Use social media to quickly get the word out about crime or suspicious activity or see who's interested in organizing a Neighborhood Watch. Ask questions that will start a conversation: Who knows a reliable baby-sitter? Can someone recommend a painter or a printer or a plumber? Ask for help with tutoring. Give away an old bicycle.

There's one piece of technology that will help you more than any other: a good old-fashioned pencil. Use it to jot a note whenever you do have that personal conversation with a neighbor. Write down their name, address, the dog's name—keep a record of what you talked about, when you met, any tidbit of trivia you can follow up on later. It's not creepy to ask if the begonias bloomed or how they enjoyed their beach vacation—it's thoughtful and kind. People remember being remembered.

Technology makes it easy to connect online, but our goal is to connect in real life.

## Meet My Neighbor

Kathy called me a few minutes after I left an invitation for coffee on her unanswered door. "I guess I'm your neighbor?" she said hesitantly. "I live on Rosewood Drive? I don't know very many people here. I'm sick. I'm waiting for a double lung transplant. I've been very isolated because of my illness."

Kathy was in tears as she thanked me for the invitation. "You don't know how much it means to me that someone thought of me and wants to be my friend."

Several months after my first conversation with Kathy, a boy appeared on my doorstep holding a greeting card. "I am delivering this on behalf of your neighbor, Kathy," he said rather formally. "If you have a moment, she is in the driveway." Lacking strength to come inside, Kathy sat in the driver's seat of her Buick while I leaned in the window and we chatted like good friends. Her daughter and son-in-law have been to my home, and I stop by to visit her.

I drove past Kathy's home an average of four times a day for seven years, squandering more than ten thousand opportunities I was given to love my neighbor. I believe the Lord will hold me accountable for driving past Kathy's pain, walking by her loneliness, and ignoring her need.

"Amy, Amy, my beloved Amy," I hear Him say. "What did you do for my daughter Kathy? I placed you within seven hundred feet of her front door at the very moment she would be reaching for me in her time of greatest need. Were you there for Kathy? Did you help her find me?"

From one man he made all the people of the world. Now they live all over the earth. He decided exactly when they should live. And he decided exactly where they should live.

Acts 17:26 NIrV

God has carefully placed us in our neighborhoods. He planned your neighborhood long before your Homeowner's Association Handbook or regional zoning committee. He planted you on your street, on your block, in your house for a specific reason, which is explained in the next verse:

God did this so that people would seek him. Then perhaps they would reach out for him and find him. They would find him even though he is not far from any of us.

Acts 17:27 NIrV

The reason God is not far from our neighbors is that He is in *each one of us*. He lives right next door, at your house! Each of us will have to stand before Him and tell Him how we loved our neighbors. There is someone in your little corner of the world who is literally *dying* to hear about Jesus.

Jesus loves your neighbors.

He stepped down from heaven to save them.

All you have to do is walk across the street to meet them.

## Next Best Steps

1. Is your neighborhood neighborly? Are you a good neighbor? Is your neighborhood friendly, or are you merely polite? Perhaps your neighborhood is decidedly unfriendly, or even dangerous. Do you have friends in your neighborhood?

2. What assumptions have you made about your neighbors? Are these judgments based on personal interaction or casual observation?

3. Do due diligence by learning about your neighbors on Facebook, Instagram, Twitter, Pinterest, etc. Then log off your computer and do something in real life. Displace a fraction of the time you spend online with real, live social interaction in the original social network: your neighborhood. How do you feel about meeting your neighbors face to face? Does initial excitement change to stress when you press the "sign out" button?

4. Do you use social media in healthy moderation? Does your family ever complain about how much you use your phone, computer, or tablet? Have you ever felt ignored or rejected because someone wouldn't get off their phone? The next time you're in a social situation—whether it's the dinner table, the lunch line, or a fast-food joint—leave your phone behind and focus on the faces in front of you.

5. Read Matthew 22:37–40 and Matthew 7:12. Jesus said these commands (love God, love your neighbor, the Golden Rule) summarize the essence or heart of everything else written in the entire Bible. Measure your investment in your neighborhood in minutes, dollars, sweat, and prayers. Is your life in sync with God's command?

6. Read John 20:11–18. In verse 16, Mary recognizes Jesus when He calls her by name. Recall a time when someone knew your name (or did not know your name) and how it made you feel. Practice using your neighbor's name in a conversation this week. What happened?

# Home Sweet Home

Every time my neighbors did laundry, my yard filled with soapy water. We shared a fence line but had never shared a conversation until the day I knocked on their door to complain. The woman who answered quickly deferred to her husband, an intimidating and rather grumpy looking man named Bill, who came outside with me to survey the sudsy situation. As we watched the water steadily trickle into my yard, Bill simply shrugged and said, "If this was my yard, I wouldn't like it. I'll take care of it." Although it cost them several thousand dollars to repair their system, Bill and Betsy proved to be conscientious neighbors.

The only time I had been inside Bill and Betsy's home was before they moved in during a realtor's Open House. The poor realtor must have known that several of his visitors (and many of his website hits) would be nosy neighbors like me![1] Of course, I was curious about how their house compared to ours in terms of size, style, and value—but I really wanted to see if it had a view into my house. We were separated by our lawns, a fence, and some trees, but our kitchen windows faced each other. Satisfied that my neighbors couldn't be too neighborly and see everything that happened in my house, I hadn't approached their front door again—not even to greet the family who moved in.

The previous owners had been strangers to me, and my "new" neighbors had lived there four or five years before the bubbly backyard dilemma forced our introduction . . . and I doubt we would have met otherwise. Betsy attends church faithfully, but she doesn't go to *my* church. We didn't have children the same age so we wouldn't have met at the park . . . besides, my neighborhood doesn't have a park. We don't have a corner coffee shop where we can conveniently bump into people. We don't have sidewalks or walking trails or bike paths. We didn't have a community building, Homeowner's Association, or Neighborhood Watch.

What we have are attached garages with doors that slide shut as soon as our cars are safely inside. We do our laundry inside and play our games inside and exercise inside. Our homes have become fortresses instead of friendly gathering places, and walled-in backyards have replaced welcoming front porches as desirable selling features.

"These suburbs—with our big houses and our big yards—became the new vision of utopia," says Dr. Danny Avula, deputy director of the Richmond City Health Department in Virginia. "These front porches where we used to sit and connect with our neighbors gave way to back decks with privacy fences where we could keep to ourselves. We could drive into our neighborhoods, into our driveways and into our garages, and walk into our houses without ever having to talk to or even see another person."[2]

With the ice broken and the drain mended, Betsy and I talked a couple more times. One weekend we collaborated to host yard sales on the same day. When my church challenged my husband and me to host a Bible study in our home and—*egad!*—invite a neighbor or two, I thought of Bill and Betsy. Would they come? Would they like it? Would they like *me*? There was only one way to find out, so I knocked on that door again, bravely faced Bill's blusteriness, and invited my neighbors to Bible study. Betsy said yes!

When Betsy came to my home the first few times, she was shy and didn't share a whole lot. But soon her quick wit and wisdom emerged, and I learned that when Betsy spoke, I'd better listen! Beneath her shyness was a comic genius who always made me laugh and a strong woman of deep faith who always made me think. When Bill got sick, one of her only respites from being a full-time caregiver was the Bible study in my home. When Bill died, her neighbors and friends gathered around.

Betsy is a good friend and godly woman. I mean, that woman can pray! She prayed down the heavens, she prayed away sickness, she prayed with power—and she had been praying on the other side of my fence for four or five years! And my, she is a good cook! Betsy continued to come to my house for Bible study, but it wasn't long before she began hosting her own prayer luncheons. Right in my backyard!

One thing I know for sure: If I hadn't intentionally invited Betsy to my home, our relationship would never have moved past the awkward you-flooded-my-backyard stage. When I got to know her, I told her I was surprised she agreed to come to our Bible study—and she broke my heart when she replied, "I was surprised you asked."

## Bring Jesus Home From Church

Maybe you're wondering, *Why is it so important to invite neighbors to my home? My church has Sunday school and lots of different Bible studies throughout the week. Can't I just invite my neighbors to my church? Doesn't that count as loving my neighbor?*

56

Yes, it does—but it's weird. Would you invite a vegetarian to a pig roast? Would you invite the mom of preschoolers to a seminar on empty nest syndrome? We need to know our neighbors' needs before we randomly invite them to church activities. Invitations to our traditional Mother's Day teas and Christmas and Easter events are trite unless we have a meaningful, personal connection and a real relationship. Yes—you can and you should invite your neighbors to church *once you get to know them.* Inviting a neighbor to church before you know anything about them is awkward, and worse— "Answering before listening is both stupid and rude" (Proverbs 18:13 THE MESSAGE).

> Jesus didn't invite people to church.

I work at a church; I think church is amazing; I love church. Churches are built for community, whether they are stained-glass and stone cathedrals or converted warehouses with worn sofas. Your church is the perfect place for meaningful teaching, engaging worship, and incredible events. The church glorifies God and shows off His wisdom to the heavens and beyond (Ephesians 3:10). Jesus created the church; He loves and leads the church. He taught at the Jewish equivalent of "church" at the Temple in Jerusalem and the synagogues around Israel; His followers also continued to gather together in the first Christian churches after the Resurrection.

But Jesus didn't invite people to church. He didn't insist on their conversion or demand their attendance. Jesus defied religious rules and sat with sinners; in fact, Jesus was just as likely to hang out in nitty-gritty Israeli neighborhoods as the Temple or Wednesday night Torah study.

Jesus went to the homes of Matthew, the much-hated tax collector; Peter, the strong-headed fisherman; a saintly woman named Mary, her bossy sister, Martha, and their once-dead brother Lazarus; a short guy with tall questions named Zacchaeus; Simon the leper; and Jairus, a leader at the synagogue—as well as the homes of many more unnamed families. He played with their children and ate at their tables. Jesus inspired huge crowds in public places, but it was in the intimate setting of homes that His teaching came alive.

> Later, when Jesus was alone with the twelve disciples and with the others who were gathered around, they asked him what the parables meant. . . . In fact, in his public ministry he never taught without using parables; but afterward, when he was alone with his disciples, he explained everything to them.
>
> Mark 4:10, 34

Your home is where people put their feet up and let their guard down. It's where relationships go deep. There's something very different about gathering in a home instead of an institutional building. Home is where we can comfortably ask uncomfortable questions, share stories, and trade tips—it's a place for extended conversations that just don't happen in the narthex, vestibule, atrium, or coffee shop after church while children squirm and husbands' stomachs growl.

## Home Sweet Home

Here's why some of your neighbors may be more receptive to coming to your home than to your church:

**Your home is comfortable.** From finding a parking space to finding the bathroom, it can be intimidating to visit a new church. It's awkward for your neighbor to walk in alone. Will their children like it? When are they supposed to stand up, sit down, raise their hands, or kneel? Are there things people who aren't members aren't allowed to do, like take communion or say *Amen*? What should they wear? Is there a secret handshake?

Will they be singled out as a visiting sinner? While it may be daunting to spend time with a neighbor they don't know well, at least they know how to behave in someone's home—so long as they keep their feet off the furniture, they're probably okay. Your home may look a little different from your neighbor's, but it is more comfortable and less threatening than a church.

**Your home is nonconfrontational.** It's sad to admit, but some women have been wounded by the church. You may be inviting them back to a place where they didn't experience the acceptance or forgiveness they craved. They may be scarred by the haughtiness, hypocrisy, or hostility they've encountered. Some of your neighbors may have been bored to tears or worked to death at church. If they've never been to church, they may have a bad impression of the people and practices they've seen portrayed in the media. But unless they've flooded your backyard, your neighbors probably feel relatively secure coming to your home. And if there are any fences that need mending between you and your neighbors, a sweet dose of hospitality can be the beginning of reconciliation.

> Your home may look a little different from your neighbor's, but it is more comfortable and less threatening than a church.

**Your home is convenient.** Some women can't squeeze another appointment onto their crowded calendars, but they can carve out time for a cup of coffee. Neighbors don't have to commute across town or find a parking place to visit your home, and a quick chat on the front porch over a glass of sweet tea is more appealing than putting on control-top hose for a ladies' tea. Convenient neighborhood friendships make life easier as well as safer—neighbors can drop in when they take the dog out, or come running when you're dangling from a ladder while cleaning the gutters. By definition, your neighbors live in the same proximity as you (remember *proximus*?)—you're just a stone's throw away, which comes in pretty handy when you need to borrow a pizza stone or the proverbial cup of sugar. As Proverbs 27:10 says, "Don't leave your friends or your parents' friends and run home to your family when things get rough; better a nearby friend than a distant family" (THE MESSAGE).

**Your home is a curiosity.** Do you ever watch those house hunter shows on television? I love to see how other people decorate and see what houses are like in different parts of the country. We're naturally curious about other people's homes: *What are they like inside? How are they like ours? How are they different?* We go to Open Houses in our neighborhoods and snoop at yard sales, so an invitation to actually come inside is practically irresistible!

**Your home simply isn't church.** Many of your neighbors already have wonderful church homes. When you gather in different homes instead of trying to get everyone to go to the same church, you will learn about other exciting ministries in your community. Neighborhood friendships build unity between churches as women from different congregations form friendships that cross denominational lines. Baptists and Episcopalians, Lutherans and Catholics, Assemblies of God, Christian Scientists, and agnostics have all gathered in my living room together! We focus on what we have in common instead of arguing about what we do differently. We share various events and opportunities sponsored by different churches; we've also found new places to volunteer like food pantries and free stores.

## Open House, Open Heart

Enough of the guilt trip already: We know we should love our real neighbors, the people right next door. But how can we bridge the gap between *conviction* about loving our neighbors and actually having real *relationships?* How do we transition from wishful thinking about loving our neighbors to having women sipping coffee around our kitchen tables? We need Martha Stewart to team up with Billy Graham to write *Loving Your Neighbors for Dummies*!

> **We need Martha Stewart to team up with Billy Graham to write Loving Your Neighbors for Dummies!**

I wasn't meeting people in my neighborhood by happenstance, so I literally knocked on their doors and invited them over for coffee at an Open House. Open Houses used to be much more common, especially at Christmastime, but today they're mostly used by realtors when people are moving *out* of a neighborhood. Why wait to have an Open House until you're closing up and moving away? The perfect time to open your home is when you're still living in it! I host an Open House once or twice a year, usually in January or September, and I enjoy the efficiency of meeting many neighbors at once. I serve coffee and cookies on paper plates—nothing fancy.

I don't ask for an RSVP to my Open Houses, so I never know how many people to expect. I want my neighbors to feel like they can stop in even if they haven't called me—and besides, I've found that RSVPing is a lost art. Good luck with that! Many people have told me they will come but don't; others' arrival is a pleasant surprise. I'm also surprised at how many women tell me they've saved all my invitations and love knowing there's an opportunity for friendship in our neighborhood, even though they've never come! Neighbors will often call or stop by to thank me for inviting them, but they don't attend.

At my first Open House, my neighbor Natalie candidly said, "I call myself a Christian, but I don't really do anything *religious*. I own a Bible but I've never read it. For me to even open a Bible would be a big deal. I see people who have faith go through things like I've gone through—and even worse—but they seem to have a hope that I don't have. I know I can get it, but I don't know how. I don't even know where to start." Well, she started in my living room.

I had one last Open House invitation in my hand when I arrived at Juanita's home. To be honest, I was dead tired and didn't want to knock on another door. But Juanita had just moved in a few days before, and the timing was perfect to invite her over. As I explained the invitation, she threw her hands in the air and yelled, "Hallelujah!" She had been praying to meet her new neighbors, but I am the one who is blessed by this faithful woman of God living across the street.

## How to Meet Your Neighbors

If you aren't meeting your neighbors in the course of everyday life, you must create opportunities yourself. Here are other activities you might consider starting in your neighborhood, with the goal of making acquaintances who become friends:

**Walking Club:** Meet at your house at a designated time, or pick people up along a pre-established route. Plan a route with several laps so people of various fitness levels can jump off early or join a little later so you all finish together. Provide water and protein bars.

**Book Club:** Choose a popular title or topic with widespread interest such as a local author or historical event, literary classic, fiction, humor, hot topic, or book that has been turned into a movie. Your book needn't be distinctly "Christian," but carefully research the content to make sure it's not offensive. Most books come with discussion questions, or you can make up your own.

**Gardening Club:** I have a black thumb, so I'd love one of my neighbors to start this! Trade seedlings, plant cuttings, divide perennials, and share your garden tools and tips. Organize a neighborhood beautification project or plant flowers at a local park. Spend an hour weeding each other's flower beds, or help at the home of a neighbor who can't care for theirs.

**Cooking Club:** Experiment with new recipes, techniques, or ingredients together. Invite a local chef to do a demonstration in your home. Or organize a freezer meal co-op: one meeting is spent selecting freezable recipes, then each participant makes enough of one recipe to give each member a serving. Meet again in several weeks to trade entrees and pick new recipes. Cook a little extra for new moms or grieving families, all while saving money and time in the kitchen.

**Scrapbooking or Card-Making Club:** Share your scrapbooking tools and use up extra supplies—and get inspiration from other creative neighbors—at a scrapbooking or card-making party. Plan one project to do together or let everyone work on their own albums, digital projects, gifts, or greeting cards. Provide plenty of tables, counter space, or lap boards, play soft music, and let the creative juices flow!

**Neighborhood Watch:** Become involved in an existing neighborhood watch program in your area and attend all the meetings. If there isn't one, contact your local sheriff or police department to learn about starting one yourself. These programs go well beyond public safety as neighbors collaborate on community concerns and look out for each other.

**Block Party:** Organize a block party and enlist several other neighbors to help out. Pass out a flyer two or three weeks in advance. Ask if anyone has folding tables and make sure people bring chairs and their own paper/plastic dishware. Provide a grill and have people bring their own meat and a dish to share (assign side dishes or desserts based on even or odd house numbers). Don't forget ice and drinks and a few fun games like a beanbag toss. Create your own icebreaker with a customized Block Party Bingo game: Find neighbors to fill in the squares with questions like "Lived here less than a year" or "Has a dog" or "Does not live on my street." Ask local businesses to donate door prizes. Many cities have a budget for block parties, so contact your local mayor's office or other appropriate local agency to find out if any financial support is available.

**Pizza Potluck:** Invite your neighbors to bring their favorite pizza—restaurant, homemade, or store-bought—to share. Most pizza shops are happy to donate coupons to pass out at your event! Divvy up responsibility to provide drinks and paper products, and ask for a few salads or desserts, too. Host the party at your home, in the driveway, or invite the whole block.

**Game Night:** Organize a family game night with board games or video games for all ages. Provide a few prizes from a dollar store. This is a great way to get together in the winter months when we don't run into our neighbors outside as often.

**Holidays:** Decorate cookies and read the Christmas story, or host an Easter egg hunt and share the Easter story. Organize a Fourth of July parade around the block or a Memorial Day picnic. Hold a bike decorating contest for kids or have a front porch decorating contest to make your entire neighborhood festive.

**Community Yard Sale:** Invite your entire neighborhood to have yard sales on the same day. Place free ads on Craigslist or pool a few dollars from participants for a paid ad. Make or purchase signs that say "Community Yard Sale This Saturday" that can be reused year after year. Check with local agencies for any restrictions on yard sales in your area. Make sure to always visit yard sales in your neighborhood so you can meet your neighbors!

## What's an Introvert to Do?

And yes, in case you're wondering, I am an extrovert. Meeting new people and hearing their stories is energizing for me. I like to make things happen, and sometimes I act hastily. What's an introvert to do? Many people prefer doing things alone or with a few close friends they feel comfortable with. They're deep thinkers, and sometimes they are slow to act.[3]

There's no exception clause to the "love your neighbor" command, so we know God designed each personality type to obey in their own unique and wonderful way. The thoughtful, introspective, sensitive, and imaginative introverts among us—as well as our introverted neighbors!—will greatly appreciate these intimate approaches to neighboring:

**Do a favor:** Call a neighbor the next time you're going to the grocery store, post office, hardware store, or mall and offer to pick up any items they might need. Better yet, invite them to come along. Doing an activity together provides just the right amount of interaction and distraction while you get to know each other.

**Make a call:** A simple telephone call can make a big difference. Nine out of ten older people reported that a chat on the phone helps them overcome loneliness . . . but one in four have no one to talk to.[4]

**Make a special delivery:** On a rainy day, deliver your neighbor's newspaper or mail to her door with a plate of cookies—or simply deliver a card that says, "Stay warm and dry!" Wrap your special treat on a dish you don't mind giving away, but that could be returned to you if your neighbor wants to continue the conversation.

**Ask for advice:** Ask your neighbor how she grows such beautiful flowers, who installed her new roof, or who she recommends for baby-sitting. She'll get a compliment; you'll get some great advice.

**Ask for help:** Ask if you can borrow an ingredient or a tool, or ask for a helping hand with a household task. Dependence is a hallmark of community, not an admission of weakness.

**Go on a date:** Invite your neighbor to breakfast at a new restaurant, share a buy-one-get-one-free lunch special, or take in a new movie together. The novelty of a new place or the thrill of a shared bargain are great ways to bond. Visit a museum or go to a concert, or take in a sporting event. Dates with a defined beginning and end time set expectations and ease anxieties.

**Create a neighborhood newsletter:** Start a newsletter just for your neighborhood, using written communication instead of verbal to form connections. Include local events, a recipe of the month, and opportunities for neighbors to gather. Interview a neighbor and share their personal story, and ask people to submit articles.

> There's no exception clause to the "love your neighbor" command, so we know God designed each personality type to obey in their own unique and wonderful way.

**Get physical:** Invite a neighbor or two to take a walk or go biking, hiking, skiing, bowling, skating, or horseback riding. The physical activity gives breathing space and provides natural breaks in the conversation.

Now that you've decided to engage with your neighbors around your home, and you've determined what you're going to do, there are just a few more details to pin down.

## Who to Invite? How Many?

You may drive down the same streets for years and not really know exactly how many people God has carefully placed in your neighborhood. Determine the number of potential new friends living around you so you can begin praying for them now!

- For a simple, accurate, and low-tech solution, just walk around and count the houses! Sketch a map and fill in names as you meet people.
- Use Google, Bing, MapQuest, or Yahoo Maps to zoom in on your neighborhood. If the satellite or street-level view is

available for your area, you can count each home in amazing detail. Check them all, because satellite images taken during different seasons reveal different details.

- Your county auditor or clerk of courts maintains detailed online property records. Search for your address at their website, then count the number of nearby homes.

I invited eighty-nine neighbors to my first Open House, and eighteen came. Typically, about one in five of your neighbors will respond to your invitation. This number may be higher if you extend a personal invitation to neighbors you already know, or lower if you leave invitations on the doorsteps of people you've never met.

## When to Do It?

Pay attention to the traffic patterns in your neighborhood. When do your neighbors take a walk? How long do their newspapers sit at the end of the driveway before they retrieve them? When are the lights on? When do the school buses run? When do the lawn mowers hum? Choose a time of day for your activity that matches the rhythm of your neighbors. Any time or day you choose will include some neighbors and exclude others—there's no way to find a perfect time for everyone.

When you settle on the time of day, you'll need to decide how long you'll meet. Meeting for ninety minutes allows enough time to get to know each other without taking up their entire day, or yours. Much longer than that puts a strain on everyone's calendar.

## How to Tell Them?

Your invitation can be scribbled on the back of an envelope or custom printed and elaborately embellished—whatever works for you. Ask a creative kid to type something up on a computer, or ask for help at the print counter of your local office supply store. Here are some ways to get the word out in your neighborhood:

- Deliver invitations door to door.
- Post an invitation at the community center or pool after checking any Homeowner's Association rules or restrictions.
- Ask the office at your apartment complex to make invitations available.
- Write an article for your neighborhood newsletter or website (even if you have to create these yourself!).
- Post information on your neighborhood Facebook or NextDoor group.
- Publish the event on Craigslist or Meetup.

A personal invitation delivered face-to-face is the most time-consuming yet most effective way to invite your neighbors into your life—you can stuff mailboxes, but the result won't be the same. Don't depend on depersonalized mass communication or electronic media to deliver a personal message.

Now you're ready to follow Jesus' advice: "Go out to the street corners and invite everyone you see" (Matthew 22:9).

## Not in My Backyard

You'll find more ideas and specific resources to connect with your neighbors in appendix B. Your neighborhood might be more into Bunco than Bible study. They might be gung ho about a book club . . . so long as it's not the Good Book. That's okay! So were Jesus' neighbors. Be intentional about creating relationships around your home and outside your religious circles. Find a way that feels natural to you. I guarantee opportunities for spiritual conversations will follow! It's perfectly okay to meet in coffee shops or community pools—the point is to move deliberately and consistently into real relationships with people who live around us.

Jesus didn't love us from afar. He didn't just pray for people as He walked past their homes; He went in and ate with them. He didn't just wish He could meet His neighbors; He stepped down from heaven and lived with us.

> Be intentional about creating relationships around your home and outside your religious circles.

Women will come if—*egad!*—you invite them in. Set the table for them. Open the door to your home.

They're dying to see what it looks like inside anyway!

## Next Best Steps

1. In your opinion, how is a home setting different from a church setting? Have you ever done a Bible study in a home? How was it different than the same kind of activity in a church? What are some pros and cons of each setting?

2. Do you know where your neighbors go to church? Make a list of the churches represented by your neighbors. What would happen on your street and in your community if these churches were unified and cooperating for the kingdom?

3. Which group activities sound appealing to you? Brainstorm ideas on what you might do with your neighbors. Research additional ideas in appendices A and B.

4. Which personal interactions sound best to you? Determine to do at least one of these activities in the next ten days. Record that date here: _____. Describe what happened.

5. Pray specifically for each home in your neighborhood. Print or draw a map of your neighborhood and mark each house as you pray. Sleuth for clues about the family who lives there so you can pray for their needs. Do this together with your family or enlist another neighbor to pray with you.

# Don't Be Weird

I live in the whitest city in America.

Growing up, every house on my street was filled with families that looked just like mine. There were a handful of black students in my graduating class of several hundred kids but no Hispanics, although I did know two families from India. Over twenty-five years later, not much has changed in these working-class neighborhoods in the foothills of Appalachia that are 96.3 percent Caucasian. According to NerdWallet, a financial website, two other U.S. cities are less diverse, but they are predominantly Hispanic—making Lancaster, Ohio, the whitest and third-least diverse city in the United States.[1]

It's a tragedy because we've missed out on the richness and vibrancy a diverse community offers. Surrounded by a sea of same-color faces, we didn't grow up practicing acceptance, appreciation, and openness. Undoubtedly, there is prejudice and discrimination here (as in any community)—but even the most open-minded and open-hearted people are woefully inexperienced at having meaningful interactions that cross racial and ethnic lines.

Diversity adds beauty to our neighborhoods as each family's culture and customs enhance our depth and personality. But diversity can also be a beast. Differences can divide us, dissimilarities can separate us, and a melting pot of conflict, misunderstandings, and condemnation can quickly boil over.

Loving our neighbors without being weird involves unconditional acceptance of people who are different from us. That may be weird in today's culture—even today's church culture—but it wasn't weird to Jesus. Don't you think Jesus overheard a few f-bombs around Simon's table? Do you imagine the Samaritan woman dressed modestly to go to the well? Do you wonder if there was a drunk guy telling dirty jokes at the wedding in Cana? Jesus preferred these people.

There was no condemnation. No eye roll. Just grace.

## Your Neighbors Are Weird

Let's be honest: Our neighbors are weird. Hiding that eye roll is hard sometimes. Your mailman delivers the same advertisements to everyone on your block since you have similar income levels, educational backgrounds, and demographic profiles—but the people who open that mail have vastly different worldviews. Our differences make it difficult to get along with our own families at the dinner table . . . let alone complete strangers down the block. They have different ideas about the origin of life, the meaning of life, and the existence of truth. They're different races; they come from different places; they speak different languages. They vote for different candidates. They're different religions—or no religion at all.

Most religions—including Christianity, Judaism, Islam, Buddhism, and Hinduism—teach some version of "Love Thy

Neighbor" or the Golden Rule: "Do to others whatever you would like them to do to you" (Matthew 7:12).

But does it matter? Do we do it?

To find out, researchers at Baylor University surveyed 389 religiously diverse adult Americans in a two-hundred-question online study designed to measure *allophilia,* a term coined in 2006 by Harvard professor Todd L. Pittinsky. A combination of the Greek roots meaning "love or like of the other," allophilia is the opposite of prejudice. It encompasses feelings of affection, comfort, engagement, enthusiasm, and kinship toward people who are different from you. While *tolerance* means merely putting up with people (the lack of negative feelings or actions), *allophilia* means actually *liking* them (the presence of positive feelings or actions).

The survey assessed attitudes toward "out-groups," such as African Americans, Arabs, Hispanics, gay men, lesbian women, and atheists. The results showed that people who considered themselves religious (i.e., they attended religious services, read sacred texts, and practiced prayer or meditation) had loving attitudes of allophilia toward people from different racial or ethnic groups, but not toward those who violated their *values.*[2]

We're okay if someone looks differently from us, cooks differently than us, or celebrates different holidays than us—but we draw the line when they think differently than us.

> Don't you think Jesus overheard a few f-bombs around Simon's table?

I keep looking, but I can't find an exception clause to the second-greatest commandment. There's no version that says, "Love your neighbor who thinks as yourself." The Lord is much more concerned with people's hearts than where their ancestors lived. In fact, "The Lord doesn't see things the way you see them. People judge by outward appearance, but the Lord looks at the heart" (1 Samuel 16:7).

Are Christian values important? Absolutely. Our challenge is to figure out how to share our values with people who don't share our values. It's a tricky proposition.

The apostle Peter can help. He gave specific advice for wives that contains a general principle for every woman—for every believer, for that matter:

> In the same way, you wives must accept the authority of your husbands. Then, even if some refuse to obey the Good News, your godly lives will speak to them without any words. They will be won over by observing your pure and reverent lives.
>
> 1 Peter 3:1–2

Peter is saying that husbands who do not believe *the Word* will be won over *without words* when they observe their wives' pure and reverent behavior. I tried this on my own husband. I thought if he saw me praying and going to church, he'd want to pray and go to church, too. I read my Bible every day and followed all the rules—and I helpfully pointed out when he didn't. I made church my number-one priority, even if that meant I didn't cook dinner and was gone three nights a week.

The Amplified Bible throws in a little phrase that explained why this didn't work very well for me. It says husbands who do not believe *the Word* will be won over *without words* " . . . when they observe the pure and modest way in which you conduct yourselves, together with your reverence *for your husband* . . ." (1 Peter 3:2 AMP, emphasis added).

> **We're okay if someone looks differently from us, cooks differently than us, or celebrates different holidays than us—but we draw the line when they think differently than us.**

The Amplified translation brings out a deeper truth: Husbands who don't believe *the Word* will be won over *without words* when they see how their wives treat *them* . . . not how their wives treat God. When I stopped trying to convert my husband to my way of thinking and focused on connecting in ways that were meaningful to him, his heart softened toward me—and toward God.

> Influence happens in the context of relationships.

Peter's specific advice is true in marriage, and it's a general principle we can apply to other relationships as well. It could be rephrased like this:

> Neighbors who don't believe the Word will be won over without words when they observe the pure and modest way in which you conduct yourselves, together with your reverence for your neighbors.

Only when people see how we behave toward them—not how many times a week we go to church or how pretty our prayers sound—will they care about our opinions or beliefs. Influence happens in the context of relationships. Loving our neighbors is about relationships, not religion.

## Different Strokes for Different Folks

"But my neighbor is [Jewish, Muslim, Hindu, atheist, foreign, redneck, gay, snobby, fill in the blank]," we whimper. "How can I possibly tell them about Jesus?" Our driveways seem as wide as the Great Divide.

Rockie Naser, a woman born in the Middle East now living in the Wild West, serves refugees from different countries and faiths including Buddhists, Muslims, and Hindus. Her advice can help us erase cultural barriers as we apply it to relationships with any neighbor who is different from us.

"We have a lot of misconceptions about Muslims," Rockie explained. "We think they're all terrorists and the women are oppressed—that we can liberate them. And they have a lot of misconceptions about Americans. They think women are exploited like pieces of meat, and that our lifestyles promote promiscuity and drinking. They think we're immodest, and frankly, they don't want to become like us."

Recognizing and acknowledging our private prejudices and mistaken beliefs is the first step toward our neighbor's door. Ask God to reveal any wrong ideas—on both sides of the fence—that are a barrier to relationships with your neighbors.

> We demolish arguments and every pretension that sets itself up against the knowledge of God, and we take captive every thought to make it obedient to Christ.
>
> 2 Corinthians 10:5 NIV

Once we've set aside our small-minded ideas, the next step is to make small talk. Jesus is the Master at this, and we can once again learn from His walk down the road to Emmaus: "He asked them, 'What are you discussing so intently as you walk along?'" (Luke 24:17).

Jesus approached the two men and stepped right into their conversation by asking, "What's on your mind? What's happening in your world right now?" Rockie recommends these questions you can ask your neighbors, and a few you should avoid:

> Once we've set aside our small-minded ideas, the next step is to make small talk.

- "What a lovely accent! Where is your accent from?" This carefully crafted question explicitly does not ask, "Where are *you* from?" which can be considered too personal in some cultures.

- "Your scarf/dress/head covering is beautiful (intricate, colorful, etc.)! What country is it from?" A compliment can lead to conversation when it's delivered politely and with sincere interest. Don't say, "What an unusual outfit!" or anything that could imply your neighbor looks different or unacceptable.
- "Have you traveled in the United States? How is the United States different from your country? How is the climate different here?" Be prepared to sympathize if your neighborhood is too hot, too cold, or too weird for your neighbor!
- "How long have you been here? Do you like it here? Where is your family?" Do not ask, "What brought you to this country?" Asylum seekers or trafficking victims may shut down at this probe. Be sensitive to their responses and travel gently through this conversation.
- "Will you tell me about the festival or feast you're celebrating?" Acknowledge their important religious holidays and celebrations, and ask about the history and traditions. Be curious, not condemning.
- "Will you tell me about your religion? What about your faith is most important to you?" Just as there are many different Christian denominations, there are many different sects and belief systems in other major world religions. And just as there are many non-practicing Christians, there are non-practicing people of other faiths. Don't make assumptions.
- "Will you tell me what you believe about Jesus? The Bible? Christians?" Seek to understand their beliefs before you share yours.

Until you have established relationships with your neighbors and know for certain what they believe, what they find offensive, and what they take delight in, here are some practical do's and don'ts—

- DO offer hospitality. Foreigners, refugees, and even people who have simply moved across town may be lonesome and far from their homes and families. Their greatest need is for community, inclusion, and relationships.

- DO invite them into your home.
- DO ask about their culture and religion with sensitivity, curiosity, and tact.
- DO try their food. Eating together is a secret ingredient in relationships.
- DO receive their hospitality. Being invited to someone's home is a great honor and gift.
- DON'T dress immodestly. A tank top and shorts is considered immodest in some cultures. Err on the side of modesty.
- DON'T offer alcohol or pork of any kind. They are forbidden in many religions.

Rockie offers one last piece of advice: DON'T be afraid. A spirit of fear is not from God. Don't be afraid to reach out and love your neighbor, even if—no, *especially* if—they practice a different religion.[3]

## You Are Weird

Let's be honest: Your neighbors think you're weird. The world's view of a Christian worldview is weird. The world thinks our stories are weird fairy tales and fantasies. They think it's weird to wake up early on the weekend to sing songs and listen to lectures instead of going golfing or sleeping in.

The reasons our youth are leaving the church are the same reasons our neighbors aren't coming in the first place. They think the church is narrow-minded and overprotective, sheltering people from the real world while ignoring real problems. They think we're boring people who don't have anything relevant or interesting to add to the things they're interested in, like careers or daily life. They give us an F in science for believing in creation and thinking we know all the answers. They think our views about sex are impossible standards that can't be kept. They think we're closed-minded, but they value an open mind and an open lifestyle. Finally, they think church leaves no room for doubt and isn't a place where they can safely ask serious questions.[4]

As believers, this is incredibly frustrating because we know life with God is anything but boring, stodgy, or irrelevant. It reminds me of my daughter's first visit to the Cheesecake Factory. She flatly refused to try cheesecake. I knew she would love it, but a recipe that combined "cheese" and "cake" was not something she would consider putting in her mouth. I wanted to give her a Cheesecake Pill that would take away her misconceptions and make her try it—

> Their greatest need is for community, inclusion, and relationships.

make her love it! When we've met Jesus Christ and He's changed us from the inside out, we want everyone to experience Him. We know they'll love Him! We want to give them a God Pill that will soften their hearts just long enough to take a taste—"Open your mouth and taste, open your eyes and see—how good God is. Blessed are you who run to him" (Psalm 34:8 THE MESSAGE).

But when we say, "Hey, why don't you come to church with me this Sunday?" our neighbors hear, "Hey, why don't you wake up at the crack of dawn, put on your most uncomfortable clothes, do a really awkward stand-up-sit-down-raise-your-hands-then-kneel routine at some old place that smells like stale communion crackers and doesn't have anything fresh to say about real life with a bunch of people who are hypocritical, judgmental, archaic-thinking know-it-alls?" Sure sounds fun, doesn't it?

We're going to have to enter this conversation through another door.

## Seven Open Doors

The good news is, there are lots of doors that open to conversations and eventually to relationships. These doors are the issues and interests that concern your neighbors, and you'll find them in the headlines of your local newspaper.

In today's *Eagle-Gazette*, I read about a man on trial for strangling his girlfriend, a mother of five. I read an article about the newly appointed Republican Party Chairman, and another about a church celebrating their bicentennial anniversary. I looked at pictures of our local schools' commencement ceremonies and learned about a factory shutdown that unemployed more than a thousand people without warning. Football, baseball, and golf dominated the sports pages.

Our little community has a lot going on, doesn't it? I bet yours does, too. If you could read a local paper from the city of Corinth in the year 50 AD, you'd find the same issues. That's when the apostle Paul visited Corinth, about seventeen years after Jesus' resurrection, and you can read about his experience in Acts 18 and 19.

> Paul proclaimed the kingdom of God in seven areas of culture that still shape our lives today.

Corinth was the cultural capital of the entire Roman empire in the region called Achaia (ak-hay-ah). It was about fifty miles west of Athens, Greece, and it was the most important city in the province because most of the commerce between Rome and Asia was shipped through its harbors. The city had been destroyed by the Romans in 146 BC, but by the time Paul visited almost two hundred years later, it had been completely rebuilt by Julius Caesar. There was a large mixed population of Romans, Greeks, and Jews; estimates of the population vary between 100,000 and 700,000.

There weren't any church buildings yet—those wouldn't be built for another two hundred years—so believers met in homes or halls or wherever they could. Each small congregation had its own leader who tried to steer the baby Christians away from the rowdy Corinthians. Corinth was a rich and luxurious city, but the people had a reputation for being immoral and nasty. Remember the song "Walk Like an Egyptian"? Well, to "live like a Corinthian" meant to live a life of immorality and drunkenness. At one time, there were over one thousand temple prostitutes at the Corinthian temple of Aphrodite, the Greek goddess of love.

Paul was on a mission to spread the Gospel, so what do you think he did when he arrived in Corinth? Do you think he started a local church and invited people to Sunday morning services? Do you think he developed a children's ministry, started a Vacation Bible School, or held a camp meeting? Do you think he scheduled a contemporary service and a traditional service?

Paul didn't do any of these things. Instead, Paul proclaimed the kingdom of God in seven areas of culture that still shape our lives today. These seven areas have always existed in every culture in every era, but they were labeled in 1975 by Bill Bright, founder of Campus Crusade for Christ; Loren Cunningham, founder of Youth With a Mission; and theologian, pastor, and author Francis Schaeffer.[5] They're commonly called Seven Mountains, Seven Keys, Seven Spheres, or Seven Gates. In our neighborhoods, they are Seven Doors we can walk through to connect with our neighbors over the interests and issues that affect their everyday lives.

**Family.** The first area that impacts our neighbors is family. When Paul arrived in Corinth, he found a family to stay with—Aquila and his wife, Priscilla (Acts 18:1–3). Today's definition of family includes men, women, children, mothers, fathers, married couples, never-married singles, single parents, divorcees, empty-nesters, widows and widowers, and even those in alternative lifestyles. In my local newspaper, you'll recall the story of the family torn apart by violence that left five young children without their mother.

Paul stayed with a local family, and his ministry transformed entire families.

> Crispus, the leader of the synagogue, and everyone in his household believed in the Lord. Many others in Corinth also heard Paul, became believers, and were baptized.
>
> Acts 18:8

**Government.** In Corinth, Paul even mixed it up with government officials, the next area of culture that's important in our neighborhoods. He was hauled up before the governor, and legal charges were filed against him:

> But when Gallio became governor of Achaia, some Jews rose up together against Paul and brought him before the governor for judgment. They accused Paul of "persuading people to worship God in ways that are contrary to our law."
>
> Acts 18:12–13

This is probably not how you want to interact with government today! Newspapers love government (especially at election time), and today's edition touted a newly appointed official. Government includes local, state, and federal government, elected officials, law enforcement, legal practices, and even public utilities.

**Religion.** The next area of influence is religion. Of course, Paul hung out with the religious crowd. Every Sabbath in Corinth he could be found at the synagogue, doing his best to convince both Jews and Greeks about Jesus (Acts 18:4). Over in Ephesus, Paul found some disciples, taught them about Jesus, and baptized them; he also went to the synagogue in Ephesus:

Then Paul went to the synagogue and preached boldly for the next three months, arguing persuasively about the Kingdom of God.

Acts 19:8

Their synagogue was like our churches today in that it was the center of the religious community: a place of prayer, study and education, charitable work, as well as a social center. Religion in our neighborhoods includes Christianity, of course—but don't forget that in Paul's day as well as ours it also includes other religions such as Judaism, Islam, New Age religions, Buddhism, Hinduism, and even atheism. The newspaper article about the church celebrating two hundred years of ministry in my hometown is a beautiful example of religion in modern neighborhoods.

**Education.** Paul was eventually kicked out of the religious establishment, so he moved on to the next area of culture: education. He set up shop in a school in Ephesus and held class there every day for two years. The school at Tyrannus was a Greek academic school, not a Jewish religious school.

So Paul left the synagogue and took the believers with him. Then he held daily discussions at the lecture hall of Tyrannus. This went on for the next two years, so that people throughout the province of Asia—both Jews and Greeks—heard the word of the Lord.

Acts 19:9–10

Paul had no hesitation about teaching the Gospel message in academia. Education includes preschools, public schools, private schools, home schools, career centers, higher education, teachers, administrators, school board members, English as a second language programs, literacy, and tutoring. The caps and gowns in my newspaper's photo gallery proudly showcased education in my city.

**Business.** The next area that shapes our communities is business. Paul was a tentmaker. He worked at a trade, he had co-workers and customers and suppliers and maybe even employees. Here at home, remember the story of the local factory shutdown? These laborers would have had a lot in common with the tentmakers at Paul's tent shop. Business is the activity of providing goods and services. It encompasses manufacturing, retail, service industries, food service, healthcare, energy, banking, accounting, and finance.

Paul sailed from Corinth to the city of Ephesus, a busy port city with a thriving trade. Ephesus was near the shrine of the fertility goddess whom the Greeks called Artemis and the Romans called Diana. The Temple of Artemis, with its weird many-breasted statues, was one of the Seven Wonders of the Ancient World. When Paul's followers stopped worshiping idols, the local businesses who depended on the Artemis souvenir trade were pretty ticked at him. According to the story, a silversmith named Demetrius got together all his employees and other business owners and said,

> Gentlemen, you know that our wealth comes from this business. But as you have seen and heard, this man Paul has persuaded many people that handmade gods aren't really gods at all. And he's done this not only here in Ephesus but throughout the entire province! Of course, I'm not just talking about the loss of public respect for our business. . . .
>
> Acts 19:25–27

**Arts and Entertainment.** Entertainment has always been big business and a powerful cultural influence, even in Paul's day; drama, magic, poetry, and art were very important in Greek culture. Arts and Entertainment includes theater, museums, dance, comedy, crafts, hobbies, books, writing, movies, and music. Our beloved sports pages feature modern-day entertainment on the football field, baseball diamond, and golf course.

The theater in Corinth seated 14,000 people, but 25,000 fans could pack into the theater in Ephesus, where a mob formed to protest Paul's interference with the Artemis trade:

> Soon the whole city was filled with confusion. Everyone rushed to the amphitheater.
>
> Acts 19:29

**Media.** They stormed the theater because of media, the final cultural shaper. The simple and effective use of word-of-mouth media was sufficient to get the entire city in an uproar.

> Inside, the people were all shouting, some one thing and some another. Everything was in confusion. In fact, most of them didn't even know why they were there.
>
> Acts 19:32

Yeah—the same thing definitely happens in our day and age! Media methods change rapidly as technology develops, but the definition remains the same: Media is the tool used to communicate any data for any purpose. Scratches on cave walls progressed to smoke signals and written signs, then to the printing press, and now we have email and emojis. Media communication includes my little hometown newspaper, television, radio, magazines, Internet, blogs, and social media like Facebook and Twitter.

These are the seven areas that shape your community and every other community of all time, from cavemen to Corinth to my hometown and yours: family, government, religion, education, business, arts and entertainment, and media. These are the issues and interests that affect every single one of your neighbors, and they are the doors you can walk through to start a conversation that can lead to a relationship.

Am I suggesting you get yourself arrested and start a riot like Paul? Um, no. But you could help a single mom carry in her groceries or mow her lawn. You could volunteer in your local parks or work at the polls. You could celebrate ministry with other churches. You could practice reading or do playground duty at your local school (even if you don't have children there). You could support local businesses and the companies where your neighbors work. You could go to the local ballpark and community theater productions. You could bring a fresh perspective to local media by filling your Facebook feed with good news and encouragement.

> These are the seven areas that shape your community: family, government, religion, education, business, arts and entertainment, and media.

### Don't Be Weird

It's weird to insist that everyone enter into a relationship with you through one door—the Religion Door. It's weird to approach your neighbors with an agenda. It's weird to tuck a King James thou-art-going-to-hell-unless-thou-repenteth tract into your neighbor's screen door, then run away in case they answer (true story—this happened at my house).

Knock on other doors your neighbors care about, and take interest in their interests. As you engage about issues that are important to them, you will have opportunities to talk about what's important to you—a relationship with Jesus Christ. This will happen gradually, incrementally, and perhaps achingly slowly. But it will happen relationally, effectively, and naturally.

### A Note to My Married Girlfriends

You know what would be weird? If your passion for your neighbors exceeded your passion for your husband. If you're married, and you've decided you want to do relationships differently in your neighborhood, it is essential that you have your husband's blessing. Share your ideas, learn if he has the same conviction, and talk about what this might mean for your household. As wives, our first ministry is our marriage.

> It's weird to insist that everyone enter into a relationship with you through one door—the Religion Door.

## A Note to My Churchy Girlfriends

You know what else would be weird? Preaching the Gospel in your neighborhood without the protective covering of your church. As a woman who wants to *lead* other women to Christ, it is important that you *follow* trusted spiritual authorities. Before you claim spiritual authority in your neighborhood, ask for your pastor's advice and blessing—

> We will not boast about things done outside our area of authority. We will boast only about what has happened within the boundaries of the work God has given us, which includes our working with you. We are not reaching beyond these boundaries when we claim authority over you. . . .
>
> 2 Corinthians 10:13–14

Be prepared to explain your heart for neighborhood ministry as well as your plan. Be ready to humbly receive any reproof or recommendations your church leadership offers in love. Look for women within your church who can mentor you and pray for you. Explain your vision and ask if they will support you in prayer, encouragement, and accountability. Ask your church if you can be accountable to them and if they will be your spiritual covering as you stretch into a new area of ministry.

Although neighborhood ministry takes place outside your church building, your church can be a powerful ally in prayer and partnership. You're not trying to find a substitute or replacement for church, nor are you recruiting for a specific church. Your neighbors may already belong to wonderful churches of their own, and the fellowship at your home can play a part in unifying the churches in your community.

## That's How You Know

Have you heard the joke, "How do you know if someone's run a marathon?" Don't worry, they'll tell you.

We love to talk about things that are important to us. If you spend any time talking to my friends Jenny or Adrienne, you're going to hear about their new babies. If you spend any time talking to my friend Ron, you're going to hear about his love for cars. If you spend any time talking to my husband, David, or my friend Michelle, you'll hear about their morning runs.

> Ask your church if you can be accountable to them and if they will be your spiritual covering as you stretch into a new area of ministry.

And if you spend any time talking to a person whose life has been transformed by Jesus Christ, you're gonna hear about it! Every conversation will be sprinkled with stories. Stories about how God's grace helped them forgive people who had hurt them. Stories about the power of the Holy Spirit helping them overcome temptation and make good choices. Stories about God providing exactly what they need at exactly the right moment. Stories about finding joy in unexpected places.

Ultimately, the story of what God has done in our lives will be told in a very natural way as it overflows out of who we are. As we get to know our neighbors very naturally, God will handle the spiritual stuff. He'll whisper in your ear when it's the right time to tell of His goodness. He'll smooth the way and tell you exactly what to say.

> If you spend any time talking to a person whose life has been transformed by Jesus Christ, you're gonna hear about it!

Seventeen years after Christ's resurrection, Jesus himself appeared to Paul in Corinth. Paul had been chased down, rejected, scorned, and accused in that wicked, depraved, and sinful city, when these red-letter words of our Savior jump out from the black text. Jesus said to Paul, and He reminds us today—

> Keep it up, and don't let anyone intimidate or silence you. No matter what happens—I'm with you and no one is going to be able to hurt you. You have no idea how many people I have on my side in this city.
>
> Acts 18:9–10 THE MESSAGE

Until we leave our comfortable church pews and sit on our neighbors' front porches, we will have no idea how many people God has placed in our cities who are on His side. Some of the people we meet will be Saints-In-Waiting, people who have not yet met Jesus and whose lives haven't yet been transformed by His love and power. We will be pulled out of the cozy places where everyone speaks our language and sings our hymns, and plopped into strange spaces where the language is rough and loud music booms. We'll hear things that make our hearts sink, and learn stories that make us heartsick.

This is exactly where we need to be.

# Next Best Steps

1. Is your neighborhood diverse? Describe the different people groups in your neighborhood.

2. Can you be honest about your preconceptions about your neighbors who are different from you? Ask God to reveal anything that is keeping you from loving your neighbors.

3. What do you think your neighbors think about you? Now, what do you *know* your neighbors think about you based on first-hand conversations and interactions with them? Do you make assumptions about their assumptions?

4. Read Acts 18–19 to see how Paul moved in all seven areas of culture.

5. What media is used in your community? Identify the seven areas of culture in your local media.

6. Check all occupations or interests where you have influence, experience, expertise, opportunity, or passion. Circle the one area where you have the most influence.

**FAMILY**

- ○ Singles
- ○ Married Couples
- ○ Parents
- ○ Single Parents
- ○ Divorcee
- ○ Alternative Lifestyles
- ○ Empty-Nesters
- ○ Widows
- ○ Other: _____

**GOVERNMENT**

- ○ Local Government
- ○ State Government
- ○ Federal Government
- ○ Elected Officials
- ○ Law Enforcement
- ○ Legal Profession
- ○ Public Utilities
- ○ Other: _____

**RELIGION**

- Christianity
- Islam
- Judaism
- Atheism
- New Age
- Buddhism
- Hinduism
- Other: _____

**EDUCATION**

- Preschools
- Public Schools
- Private Schools
- Home Schools
- Career Centers
- Higher Education
- Teachers
- ESL
- Literacy
- School Administration
- School Board
- Tutoring
- Other: _____

**BUSINESS**

- Retail
- Banking
- Accounting
- Lawyers
- Service Industries
- Food Service
- Manufacturing
- Healthcare
- Energy
- Finance
- Other: _____

**ARTS & ENTERTAINMENT**

- Art
- Theater
- Museums
- Dance
- Comedy
- Crafts
- Books
- Movies
- Sports
- Music
- Other: _____

**MEDIA**

- Communication
- Television
- Radio
- Newspaper
- Magazines
- Internet
- Blogging
- Social Media (Facebook, Twitter)
- Other: _____

7. Which of these areas are the most pressing concerns for your neighbors? What conversations are they having on all sides of these issues?

8. How can you get involved in these areas to make a difference and deepen relationships in your community?

9. If you're married, how does your spouse feel about relationships in your neighborhood? Will loving your neighbor be a source of conflict or collaboration in your home?

10. What did your church say when you approached them about loving your neighbor? Will they partner with you in practical and spiritual ways?

# Fears and Excuses

Last winter we learned two new words in Ohio: *polar vortex*. We're used to cold winters, but the polar vortex achieved a whole new level of misery. The coldest day dipped to -19° F with dangerous wind chills that closed schools and businesses. Frozen pipes burst and frozen people bundled up.

Of course, this is when I decided to go meet my neighbors.

As I mentioned before, I host an Open House for my neighbors once or twice a year, and it never fails that the forecast for the day I need to pass out invitations is either a polar vortex, a blizzard, unbearably hot, or raining cats and dogs. I've had to evade snowdrifts as well as sprinklers to knock on my neighbors' doors!

I have to endure the bad weather because I've usually put this off until the last possible moment. I'm a deadline-driven procrastinator who is easily distracted. If I have a difficult task I don't know how to tackle, I inexplicably find myself alphabetizing my spices, color-coding my sock drawer, cleaning out my inbox, or finally catching up on mountains of laundry. Sometimes I'll find myself in the kitchen looking for a snack—as if the answers I need are hidden inside a cookie!

When I returned from the conference where I first heard the words "neighborhood Bible study," I had a head full of ideas but a heart full of resistance. As the reality of this idea sunk in— *knocking on doors! talking to strangers! cleaning my house!*—I flinched.

I ignored the clear vision God had given me for my neighborhood and allowed myself to be sidetracked with other less-than-noble deeds. "But the noble man makes noble plans, and by noble deeds he stands" (Isaiah 32:8 NIV).

I can always find something I *need* to do when I don't *want* to do what I know I *ought* to do. I create busywork so I don't have to do big work. I do necessary and trivial things while avoiding the urgent and important things.

> I had a head full of ideas but a heart full of resistance.

Like loving my neighbors.

You'd think I would get right on it. I write about loving your neighbors. I speak about loving your neighbors. I love loving my neighbors! I've helped countless women invite their neighbors over for coffee. But still, for me—sometimes it's hard. It takes a lot of time. It's risky. It's an investment into people's lives, and that can be messy. I don't know where to start, what to say, or how to be. I'm afraid.

The thought of knocking on my neighbors' doors made my knees knock. I hid behind my logical excuses, rational defenses, and stubborn resistance.

## Flashback

When our daughter's basketball game was played at my old junior high school, flashbacks to mean girls and merciless teasing nearly gave me a panic attack. I hated junior high. Hated. It.

Friendships were awkward, classes were hard, clothes were *so* important. It was the year of the polo, and I don't mean the cheesy riderless horse on the JCPenney brand—only the mallet-wielding dude on a genuine Ralph Lauren polo would do (or the open-mouthed Izod alligator). I remember my joy and relief when my parents sacrificed the entire family's clothing budget to acquire five acceptable polo shirts for me, one for each day of the week, so I could flip my collar in style. Fitting in was my first priority, and I was desperate for acceptance.

> Obeying Christ's command to love my neighbor was as terrifying as finding a place to sit in the junior high lunchroom.

It was my fear of not fitting in that drove me to the wrong crowd. I chucked my church values out the window when they caused kids (and even teachers) to tease me. I stopped listening to my Amy Grant cassettes when my friends played Duran Duran. I started cussing when it brought a laugh. I walked away from God and ran toward the crowd, and it would be years before I returned to Him. I changed my values and my behavior to fit in.

My fears drove me to disobedience as a child, and not much changed when I was all grown up. Obeying Christ's command to love my neighbor was as terrifying as finding a place to sit in the junior high lunchroom.

My fears became my excuses, and I had every excuse in the book.

## My Fear of Sacrifice Became the Excuse "I Don't Have Time"

"I don't have time to go talk to my neighbors, make friends, invite them into my home, and figure out what we're going to

95

talk about!" I reasoned, "God has blessed me with a good job, a busy family, and many responsibilities at church. This is what He wants me to focus on for this season of my life."

In reality, I was being stingy with my time. Tithing and financial giving had once been difficult for me, until I saw how God stretched my budget when I gave a small portion back to Him. It took me a long time to make the same connection with giving Him my time.

When I argued that I didn't have time, God showed me who was *really* in control of my calendar.

- My work was fraught with setbacks and struggles that felt overwhelming.
- At home, I couldn't keep my house clean or get dinner on the table.
- I wasn't able to go to family get-togethers and I missed out on girlfriend time because of pressing chores or deadlines.
- I couldn't volunteer at our daughter's school or our church like I wanted.
- My worship was dry; my personal time with God was practically nonexistent.

> **When I argued that I didn't have time, God showed me who was really in control of my calendar.**

For every minute I hoarded, two more were wasted on silly goof-ups and dumb mistakes.

I was afraid to lay my daily planner on the altar. I wanted to make my own plans and be in charge of my own day.

But an amazing thing happened when I finally made the time to get to know my neighbors: God magnified each minute. I became productive, resourceful, capable, energetic, and effective again. Work eased up; the house stayed straightened. I had breathing room to visit with friends . . . and some of those friends were my neighbors!

## My Fear of Humiliation Became the Excuse "I'm Not Spiritual Enough"

"If my neighbors find out I'm a Christian, they'll expect me to know the answers to life's toughest questions. They'll ask how a loving God could send people to hell, or why children get sick. They'll demand to know if there are dinosaurs in the Bible and make fun of me because I believe in Noah's Ark. I'm not ready for this. I still get Zephaniah and Zechariah mixed up, and I haven't read the whole Bible."

I believed that before you begin to love your neighbor, you must be perfectly prepared. Your house must be spotless, your children spit-shined. You must not be fighting with your husband or the teller at the bank. You must memorize all the books of the Bible and pass a course on apologetics. . . .

Oh, no—I just disqualified myself. Let's start over.

Before you begin to love your neighbor, you must have a sincere desire to love your neighbor because you love Jesus.

I rationalized that I wasn't ready to love my neighbor because I didn't have all the answers. You don't have to have all the answers! The more honest and vulnerable you are, the more your neighbors will respect you. People don't trust anyone who acts like, "I'm perfect, and if you hang out with me you can be perfect too." But they relate to vulnerability, honesty, and transparency. Here's an amazing thing I've discovered: People are more impressed by God's full provision for my sins than they are with any fake perfection I try to cover them up with.

> I was afraid to lay my daily planner on the altar.

You are already ready to love your neighbor! You're smart enough and you're spiritual enough. You don't have to act all super-spiritual, just be yourself (even if you really are super-spiritual!).

> You don't have to have all the answers! The more honest and vulnerable you are, the more your neighbors will respect you.

By the way, I've never had a neighbor (or anyone else for that matter) ask these kinds of questions with the expectation that I would know all the answers immediately . . . if ever. These are the dilemmas that keep people up at night and keep them from trusting God. If you're on the hook, try this:

- Restate the question to be sure you've understood correctly.
- Ask questions about their question. Ask what they think. Ask why they're asking.
- Admit you don't know. Say, "I don't know the answer to that. Your question is so important to me, may I have some time to think over my response?"
- Ask if you can meet again to talk about it later.

It may be scary, but it's actually an honor to be trusted with difficult conversations.

## My Fear of Vulnerability Became the Excuse "I Have a Shady Past"

"I fight with my husband and get mad at stupid drivers—I love personalized license plates so that I can scold people by name! I used to smoke and cuss and many, many worse things that some of my neighbors probably know about. They saw my dirty look when their dog dug up my flowers. I have a bad reputation."

I hope I'm not giving anything away here, but people "in ministry" have deep, dark closets that hold lots of skeletons.

So, yeah, I smoked—for twenty years! I've been on the brink of divorce and financial disaster. I'm pretty sure I've ruined my daughter with my less-than-stellar parenting skills. I yell at other drivers (come on, you're with me!) and I don't spend enough time with my mother. There are still more skeletons rattling in my closet, clacking bones that keep me awake at night. They make my confession of smoking as innocuous as cute kitten videos.

> It's not a life of perfection that prepares you for ministry, but an abundance of God's grace.

Good thing it's not a life of perfection that prepares you for ministry, but an abundance of God's grace. The apostle Paul said,

> I thank Christ Jesus our Lord, who has given me strength to do his work. He considered me trustworthy and appointed me to serve him, even though I used to blaspheme the name of Christ. In my insolence, I persecuted his people.
>
> 1 Timothy 1:12–13

The skeletons in Paul's closet were that he blasphemed the name of Christ and persecuted the church. Knowing your imperfect past, God also considers you trustworthy and appoints you to serve Him—even though you used to _____ [fill in the blank].

No matter what you did yesterday, God can use you today. He uses imperfect people to accomplish His perfect plan every day! After repentance and restoration, after listening and learning, nothing and no one is ever wasted! Paul continues,

> But God had mercy on me because I did it in ignorance and unbelief. Oh, how generous and gracious our Lord was! . . . He

filled me with the faith and love that come from Christ Jesus. This is a trustworthy saying, and everyone should accept it: "Christ Jesus came into the world to save sinners"—and I am the worst of them all.

1 Timothy 1:13–15

I competed for the title of "World's Worst Sinner" for a long time—and I don't think I'm done yet: I manage to mess up daily! Paul gives me hope despite my bumbling as he wraps up this passage with praise and a promise:

> But God had mercy on me so that Christ Jesus could use me as a prime example of his great patience with even the worst sinners. Then others will realize that they, too, can believe in him and receive eternal life. All honor and glory to God forever and ever! He is the eternal King, the unseen one who never dies; he alone is God. Amen.

1 Timothy 1:16–17

I am a good example of a bad example. The beauty of my ugliness is that Christ uses it as an example of His patience! My story is for His glory, and it's a tale of grace, forgiveness, and redemption. Like a cracked streetlight, God shines through the cracks of my brokenness and casts a unique light on my neighborhood.

## My Fear of Rejection Became the Excuse "My Neighbors Aren't Spiritual"

A sweet retired man in my hometown has given hundreds of white wooden crosses to anyone who asks, and they are proudly displayed in flower beds around the city. There's a good chance you're a heathen if you don't have a cross in your yard. I counted the number of crosses in my neighborhood and concluded that most of my neighbors don't have a spiritual bone in their bodies. It would be a waste of time to try to start a spiritual conversation.

It's one thing to approach a complete stranger or brief acquaintance and talk about the weather—that's already a big step. But it's quite another thing to talk about faith and heaven and sin and weighty, eternal stuff. Won't my neighbors be offended? Won't they think I'm rude? The answer is, simply: Yes. They might be offended. They might think you are rude. They might think you are out of your mind! And they might be right. It *is* offensive and rude to shove your agenda before you've shown your love. Spiritual conversations must begin with natural relationships.

> It is offensive and rude to shove your agenda before you've shown your interest. Spiritual conversations must begin with natural relationships.

We cannot take a neighbor's rejection personally if they reject God spiritually. All we're called to do is share God's love—whether or not they accept it is between them and God.

> I never shrank back from telling you what you needed to hear, either publicly or in your homes. I have had one message for Jews and Greeks alike—the necessity of repenting from sin and turning to God, and of having faith in our Lord Jesus. . . . I declare today that I have been faithful. If anyone suffers eternal death, it's not my fault, for I didn't shrink from declaring all that God wants you to know.
>
> Acts 20:20–21, 26–27

We aren't responsible for our neighbors' response, but only for our actions. Every single one of our neighbors will spend eternity in heaven or hell, whether they realize it or not. They may not be religious, but they are definitely spiritual!

## My Fear of Comparison Became the Excuse "My House Isn't Nice Enough"

"My furniture is worn. My holy dog sniffs people in unholy places. I've been meaning to paint the living room like this one I saw on TV and in those shiny magazines. What will people think?"

Confession: My house is not Pinteresting. I've never made a pennant banner, and I don't own spray paint or Mod Podge. Seriously, did God know about Pinterest when He told us to love our neighbor? Didn't He know we'd break out in a cold sweat at the thought of creating the perfect centerpiece and folding our napkins like swans?

> Seriously, did God know about Pinterest when He told us to love our neighbor?

As a woman, wife, and mother, I know how important our homes are. It might be old-fashioned, but I still think of myself as the keeper of my house—and I do want it to be nice. I just have to be careful that my natural desires don't clash with Christ's command. It's tempting to compare my lived-in house to touched-up, professionally staged rooms that are Photoshopped more than a swimsuit cover model.

> Don't love money; *be satisfied with what you have*. For God has said, "I will never fail you. I will never abandon you." So we can say with confidence, "The Lord is my helper, so I will have no fear. What can mere people do to me?"
>
> Hebrews 13:5–6 (emphasis added)

Just for fun, I searched "Be satisfied" on Pinterest and found thousands of images that made me anything but! The majority were delicious, decadent, fattening foods. The rest were shiny new shoes, chic clothes, sexy hairstyles, exotic travel destinations, and steely abs. In chapter 9, we'll talk about caring for our homes so they can be a blessing to our neighbors. We have a responsibility to be presentable, but we're not called to be perfect.

## My Fear of People Became the Excuse "I Might Get Hurt"

"You just can't be too careful. If I went up to my neighbor's house, I could be assaulted, kidnapped, shot, or maimed. It's a dangerous world."

Some neighbors are dangerous. Some situations are explosive. Each night, Google sends me a list of every news headline with the word *neighbor* in it. There are just as many stories of neighborhood disputes as there are stories about neighbors saving each other's lives.

We should take commonsense safety precautions when approaching an unfamiliar home. Women should talk to women, men should talk to men. Take a friend with you. Make sure someone knows where you are and when you'll be home. Take your phone. But here's the bottom line: There is no foolproof way to protect yourself from evil people.

Well, then. I guess we'll just have to trust God. This whole "love your neighbor" thing was His idea, anyway.

The Israelites were afraid to trust God when they felt physically threatened. Twelve spies cased out the neighborhood God had promised to give them, and they returned with conflicting reports. Ten of them spread this bad news:

> We can't go up against them! They are stronger than we are! . . .
> The land we traveled through and explored will devour anyone
> who goes to live there. All the people we saw were huge. We
> even saw giants there, the descendants of Anak. Next to them
> we felt like grasshoppers, and that's what they thought, too!
>
> Numbers 13:31–33

The Promised Land was full of threatening, imposing, ginormous beasts who would trample the Israelites just as easily as stomping on a bug. This dire warning sent the entire community into a frenzy of weeping and crying, moaning and complaining. In their panic, they wanted to kill Caleb and Joshua, the two spies who voiced a different opinion:

> Do not rebel against the Lord, and don't be afraid of the people of the land. They are only helpless prey to us! They have no protection, but the Lord is with us! Don't be afraid of them!
>
> Numbers 14:9

Caleb and Joshua didn't deny that the people were giants. They didn't pooh-pooh the possible danger. They would go on to fight many battles with the Anaks and other bigger, stronger tribes. But they saw the bigger picture when they faced a bigger enemy: God was with them. They recognized that shrinking back in fear is simply rebellion against God.

"The Lord is with us! Don't be afraid of them!" With those ten words, all my excuses went out the window.

## True Confession Time

Can I just be honest? The real reason I didn't love my neighbor is because I'm lazy.

All my fears, my many excuses, my justifications, and my rationalizations were convenient cover-ups for the cold, hard truth: I didn't want to love my neighbor. Nope. No way. It was too hard. It's too much to ask. I didn't want to give up my right to myself—my time, my life, my home. I was selfish and lazy. These synonyms for *lazy* are hard to swallow: apathetic, careless,

> Shrinking back in fear is simply rebellion against God.

inattentive, indifferent, passive, asleep on the job, dallying, idle, indolent, neglectful, remiss, slack, sluggard, unconcerned, unready. I have been all these and more to my neighbors.

"The lazy person claims, 'There's a lion out there! If I go outside, I might be killed!'" (Proverbs 22:13). Lazy people make up crazy excuses. There *is* a lion out there, the devil—and he is prowling our neighborhoods looking for someone to devour (1 Peter 5:8). Here's what I forgot: That puny lion can be defeated by a stronger Lion!

> Lazy people make up crazy excuses.

"The wicked run away when no one is chasing them, but the godly are as bold as lions" (Proverbs 28:1). The Proverbs are full of pithy verses about my laziness and its devastating impact on my neighborhood:

- Lazy people are irritating to those they are supposed to serve (Proverbs 10:26).
- Lazy people don't get the results they want (Proverbs 13:4).
- Lazy people face unforeseen obstacles (Proverbs 15:19).
- Lazy people destroy things (Proverbs 18:9).
- Lazy people's own needs won't be met (Proverbs 19:15).
- Lazy people live in neglected neighborhoods (Proverbs 24:30–34).

Check, check, and check! I felt the painful consequences of my laziness in my faith, my family, my finances, my work, and my neighborhood. This was the result of my refusal to love my neighbor—

One day I walked by the field of an old lazybones, and then passed the vineyard of a lout; They were overgrown with weeds, thick with thistles, all the fences broken down. I took a long look and pondered what I saw; the fields preached me a sermon and I listened: "A nap here, a nap there, a day off here, a day off there, sit back, take it easy—do you know what comes next? Just this: You can look forward to a dirt-poor life, with poverty as your permanent houseguest!"

Proverbs 24:30–34 THE MESSAGE

A run-down neighborhood with overgrown weeds and broken fences isn't just bad for property values: It's bad for people. When I felt overwhelmed with all I could do in my neighborhood, I needed this reminder of God's words to those lazy Israelites as they prepared to enter His Promised Land with its many dangers, toils, and snares:

So be strong and courageous! Do not be afraid and do not panic before them. For the Lord your God will personally go ahead of you. He will neither *fail* you nor abandon you.

Deuteronomy 31:6 (emphasis added)

This word in this verse that is translated "fail" is the same one that is translated as "lazy" in Proverbs 18:9. God will not be lazy. He will not let us down, He will not leave our neighborhood, and He will personally go ahead of us. Kinda like Jesus, when He told the disciples to go into new neighborhoods with the Gospel:

The Lord appointed seventy others also, and sent them two by two *before His face* into every city and place *where He Himself was about to go.* Then He said to them, "The harvest truly is great, but the *laborers* are few; therefore pray the Lord of the harvest to send out laborers into His harvest."

Luke 10:1–2 NKJV (emphasis added)

God sends us before His beautiful face to the very cities and places where He himself intends to go. Because of my laziness, Jesus had to enter my neighborhood on potholed streets. He came to dilapidated shacks. He arrived at homes too poor to offer Him a meal.

Jesus saw the harvest of souls on our streets, and He prayed for laborers to work these ripe fields. By definition, laborers are the opposite of lazybones. The Greek root word of laborer, *ergatēs*, is where we get the word *erg*, a unit of work or energy. Laborers are diligent, energetic, hardworking, industrious. They get the job done.

And they are few.

## He Knows You Knew

When God asked me to do something I didn't want to do, I came up with a hundred reasons why it was a bad idea. Here's the best part about my excuses: They are all legit. I don't have time to love my neighbors—I don't know a single woman who does. I'm never going to have all the answers, someone will always have a nicer home than me, and I could conceivably be mugged in my own neighborhood. God must have thrown up His hands and sighed, "Okay, I give in, you're right. But what about me? Didn't I create time? Don't I know everything? Didn't I choose your home? Don't I protect you? What am I, chopped liver?"

I'm looking for that exception clause again, the obscure translation that reads, "Love your neighbor when it's convenient for you." God takes the command a little more seriously—

> Rescue those who are unjustly sentenced to die; save them as they stagger to their death. *Don't excuse yourself* by saying, "Look, we didn't know." For God understands all hearts, and he sees you. He who guards your soul knows you knew. He will repay all people as their actions deserve.
>
> Proverbs 24:11–12 (emphasis added)

> God sends us before His beautiful face to the very cities and places where He himself intends to go.

The Lord looks right past my weak excuses into the weary eyes of my neighbors. He has commanded us to love our neighbor, and He designed us with the ability to do it well.

## Women Helping Women

God designed women with the ability to enjoy community. We gab about everything from Crock-Pot recipes to current affairs; we talk about shoe sales and social justice. Within minutes of meeting a new girlfriend, we've been known to whisper helpful tips on marriage, menopause, and the meaning of life.

So why is it so hard to talk about Jesus?

Why can I say "God bless you" to a stranger but can't tell a friend how God blessed me? Why does my throat get dry and my palms get sweaty when the Holy Spirit nudges me to tell my neighbor about my Savior? Why can I go to church on Sunday and praise Jesus, but Monday at the mall I'm a tongue-tied mess?

Jesus, my precious Jesus, saved my life, redeemed my marriage, and restored my family. Would my testimony be reduced to a fish bumper sticker on my minivan and some Jesus jewelry?

After months of debate, delay, and disobedience, I finally decided to meet my neighbors. I've also met dozens of dogs of all shapes and sizes—I'll take dog treats with me next time! One day I met the pastor of a local church on her way to deliver meals and the owner of a local bar enjoying a beer on her front porch. I've met women in high heels and women in slippers (and a few still wearing pajamas).

You'd be surprised how many people leave their Christmas lights up year-round (one house still had a Christmas tree in the living room in the middle of summer!). Some homes are meticulous, not a leaf out of place. Others have cobwebs over the front door because families disappear into attached garages, never to be seen again.

Without exception, the women who are home invite me inside to visit (maybe the fact that I always decide to meet my neighbors during a blizzard or a heat wave has something to do with it). They are gracious and kind, even if they are uninterested in my invitation to an Open House. Only one person has refused to take the invitation from my hand (so I snuck it in her mailbox). One of my neighbors told me about myself! "There's a lady down the street who invites the neighbors over," she helpfully explained. When she described my house to a tee, I assured her it was me. "Oh, no, honey—this isn't you," she insisted.

At one home, an elderly neighbor and I shared names of families we might know in common, and she learned that someone she's been praying for on her church's prayer list lives right in her backyard—literally! She can see the other woman's house from her kitchen sink. She was praying *for* her, when she could have prayed *with* her.

> The Lord looks right past my weak excuses into the weary eyes of my neighbors. He has commanded us to love our neighbor, and He designed us with the ability to do it well.

Like a spy in the Promised Land, I offer you this final report: It's worth it. I've made true friends—women I can call to share a cup of coffee, help me hang a picture, or borrow an egg. My neighbors pray for me. I feel connected with my neighborhood. I feel safer. And I feel I've been obedient to the particular mission God has given me.

I'll try to remember that the next time I feel compelled to write out my Christmas cards or file my taxes instead of obeying Christ's command to love my neighbors.

This thing I dreaded, even as I was dreaming of it, has become my deepest joy.

# Next Best Steps

1. Do you get distracted? Keep a log of the activities that waste the time you could spend loving your neighbor. Ask someone to keep you accountable for the minutes of your day.

2. Read 1 Thessalonians 5:19. Have you ever stifled the Holy Spirit? What clear directive has He given you that you've ignored?

3. What are your personal fears and excuses about loving your neighbor? Is there actual evidence to support your fears, or are they a figment of your imagination?

4. Have you ever been put on the spot by a tough question? What was it? How did you respond? Have you been the one asking tough questions? How did others' answers draw you toward or push you away from Christ?

5. Practice sharing one aspect of your testimony. Include enough details of your shady past so that people can truly relate, but don't draw word pictures that could create temptation or cause unnecessary pain or embarrassment to others. The subject is God's grace, not the gory details.

6. Write a prayer of thanksgiving for your home—no matter how you feel about its amenities. List its positive attributes and thank God for the gift of shelter. Ask Him how you can use your home for His glory.

7. Describe the safety of your neighborhood. What commonsense steps can you take to protect yourself as you love your neighbor?

8. How many "ergs" (a unit of work or energy) do you expend in your neighborhood? What literal, visible, measurable, and practical actions have you taken to love your neighbor?

# It's All Spiritual

There is a mountain in the middle of my Midwestern town. Surrounded by gently rolling hills and flat-as-a-pancake farmland, the sandstone face of Mount Pleasant juts 250 feet in the air to dominate our skyline. You're rewarded with panoramic views of the city and picturesque county fairgrounds when you huff and puff your way to the top—on a clear day, you can even catch a glimpse of the state capital's skyline some thirty miles away.

The abundance of sandstone and natural gas in the area attracted glass manufacturers as far back as 1890, when the first glass factory hired its first worker. Today, the glass factory is the second-largest private sector employer in the city.

Or it was. Before it closed.

They didn't officially "close," but the parent company furloughed almost all of the 1,140 local employees for what they said would be a three- or four-week shutdown to cut costs and reduce inventory. The employees didn't have a few months to plan for a few weeks without income. They didn't have a plant-closing party to say good-bye to their friends and co-workers. They didn't know this was coming, and they don't know when it will end. As I write, six weeks have passed. A smaller plant in a neighboring state has been called back to work, as have a few hundred local employees here—but there was also some scary paperwork filed with the SEC that warned of a potential permanent shutdown. It's an unresolved and unsettling situation for many families, some of whom have worked there for generations and depend on the factory for more than one wage earner in their household.

Thankfully, *my* family is unaffected. We just live here. We don't work there. I know a few people who worked there many years ago, but none of my friends work there now. I won't feel much of a pinch from $875,000 in lost tax revenue for my city each year. I can take a detour around the big, ugly environmental disaster in the heart of town if the factory shuts down for good. The 33 percent increase in unemployment in my county wouldn't affect me; it only affects my neighbors.

My neighbors . . . my neighbors . . . wait a minute, didn't Jesus say something about loving our neighbors?

Of course He did, and that is why problems like this one affect us all. These aren't just economic problems. They aren't just environmental problems. They aren't public affairs. They are intensely personal affairs that are sucking the life out of individuals, families, and entire neighborhoods.

My little city stepped up in a big way. Task forces were formed to quickly match people with financial assistance, food, and medical care. Employees could show their badges and get discounts on pizza, haircuts, and even dog grooming at sympathetic businesses. Grassroots groups collected diapers, toiletries, and cleaning supplies—items in short supply at food pantries—and delivered them to affected families. Facebook groups popped up where people could post special needs—a pair of pants to wear to graduation, infant formula. The Salvation Army food pantry closed its doors when demand exceeded supply, but quickly reopened when caring citizens quickly responded with donations of food and cash.

Local pastors pooled their people and pulled out all the stops to host a "We Care" rally across the street from the factory. The entire community was invited for free hot dogs and bottled water, bounce houses, sno-cones and popcorn, face painting, and free kids' games. Government agencies and charitable organizations set up tables to pass out information and take expedited applications for assistance, and a prayer tent was available for people seeking spiritual support and encouragement. When the newspaper covered the rally,

> Why is it news when people pray? Because loving our neighbors is a big deal.

other local businesses called to see how they could help; they donated food and brought volunteers, then stayed to clean up. Hundreds of neighbors gathered on a public school playground where the rally was held as civic leaders and pastors from different churches prayed for the affected families, the parent company, our city leaders, and our community of neighbors.

The mother of one of the furloughed employees made an innocent little post on Facebook about praying on the sidewalk in front of the factory, and two different television news crews showed up to film it. Why is it news when people pray? Because loving our neighbors is a big deal. A crisis can create community as God works good out of bad. I'm not glad this happened in my town, but I am forever grateful for the way it has opened our eyes—and our hearts, and our hands—to our neighbors.

The second-greatest commandment isn't an arbitrary rule put in place so God can measure, test, and score our commitment. "Love your neighbor" isn't a random command, it's God's perfect plan. When our love for Him overflows onto our neighbors, our communities will be stronger, our streets will be safer, and our neighbors will even live longer. The impact of loving our neighbors reaches much further than you might think.

## Economic Impact

Your involvement in your neighborhood can impact the economic condition of your entire community. New business ideas that will eventually provide employment and fill tax coffers are typically started by one or two people in their living room, garage, or basement. Their first customers are their neighbors, friends, and family. By knowing our neighbors' economic interests—what they do to earn a living and where they go to do it—we can support our community marketplace. Is your neighbor a mechanic? Take your car to him. Does your neighbor do alterations? Take your curtains to her. Is your neighbor a banker, a doctor, a sales clerk? Support their livelihood by supporting their employers.

> Each dollar you invest in your community blesses your neighbor.

We can support our local economy by shopping at farmer's markets, finding a local insurance agent, and frequenting locally owned businesses. I've actually heard tales—from people who are still alive!—of being able to find everything you needed for your household within a short drive of your home, provided by people you knew personally. Before big box stores crowded out mom and pop shops, consumers and merchants had a personal relationship. Decisions about factory closures and the fate of countless families weren't made in far-away board rooms. Networking didn't happen online; it happened at lunch counters. Product selection was based on conversations in the hardware aisle, not computer-generated algorithms. People found jobs because a friend personally recommended them, not through online application pools.

We can also love our neighbor by financially investing in local schools, parks, roads, and infrastructure. We have paid private school tuition for our daughter's entire education, yet I supported a school levy to build five desperately needed new public schools. I saw this as a special opportunity to love my neighbors, their children, and the future children in my community.

> Wherever your treasure is, there the desires of your heart will also be.
>
> Matthew 6:21

Each dollar you invest in your community blesses your neighbor, whether she is a business owner, employee, or the beneficiary of benefits provided by local taxes.

## Safety Impact

An economically challenged community is at greater risk for crime. A 2002 study at The Ohio State University showed that when unemployment goes up, so do crimes like burglary and theft of personal property. A New Zealand study found a significant link between unemployment and "dishonesty" offenses like theft, burglary, auto theft, fraud, and receiving stolen property.[1]

Do you know what impacts the safety of your community more than anything else? Is it the presence of police patrols? Is it armed security systems and motion-activated cameras? Is it Neighborhood Watch, streetlights, or gated streets? Locking your doors and windows?

Nope. The two most important things you can do to make your neighborhood safer are to get to know your neighbors' names and to get out of your house.[2] "The more neighbors interact and care about each other, the less opportunity for crime there seems to be," says Dave Bailey, Chief of Police for the Lancaster (Ohio) Police Department. "I am not saying that the police are not important here, but nothing really beats neighbors helping neighbors. Actually knowing our neighbors can give us the feeling that we have some level of responsibility for them."

If you want to live in a safer neighborhood, get to know the names of the people who live around you and do stuff with them—talk at the curb as you walk the dog, borrow tools, eat together in one another's homes. Chief Bailey adds, "These closer relationships also allow us to really know the daily rhythms of our neighborhoods, making it easier to spot suspicious activity and things that are out of place. Some neighbors seem to take ownership of their areas. They pick up trash, remove graffiti, mow lawns, and look out for the old folks. They send a signal that someone is watching."

## Wellness Impact

When you go to the doctor, you're quizzed about your family history and lifestyle—but maybe they should start asking about your zip code, too. Your neighborhood impacts your life-span and quality of life. The wealthy neighbors in Fairfax County, Virginia, have an average life expectancy of eighty-two years for men and eighty-five years for women—similar to the idyllic country of Sweden. Six hours away in McDowell County, West Virginia, men live to be an average age of sixty-four and women live to be seventy-three—the same life expectancy as war-torn Iraq.[3] When the U.S. Department of Housing and Urban Development offered low-income single mothers the chance to move out of poor neighborhoods in the 1990s, families who relocated to lower-poverty areas had less obesity and diabetes more than ten years later.[4]

Our neighborhoods affect our health because they determine our access to health care, pharmacies, preventative medical services, fresh food, and parks, sidewalks, and safe places for physical activity. The stress of poverty also plays a role in wellness. Since we can't all move out of our neighborhood or pass out fistfuls of cash to underprivileged neighbors, how can we help?

Just be nice.

Turns out, God created us with a vagus nerve—a wandering cranial nerve that passes through the heart, esophagus, and lungs on its way from the brain stem to the abdomen. The vagus nerve is part of the involuntary nervous system that regulates unconscious body processes like heart rate, blood pressure, and food digestion. Researchers at the Positive Emotions and Psychophysiology Lab at the University of North Carolina found that a form of Buddhist meditation that repeatedly wishes happiness, wellness, and peace upon others has a powerful effect on the vagus nerve.[5] (I'm no Buddhist, but this sounds a lot like Christian prayer.) The brilliance of the second-greatest command is that the act of loving our neighbors signals the vagus nerve to lower blood sugar, increase concentration, regulate emotions, and reduce inflammation, arthritis, and heart disease.

> The two most important things you can do to make your neighborhood safer are to get to know your neighbors' names and to get out of your house.

> Kind words are like honey—sweet to the soul and healthy for the body.
>
> Proverbs 16:24

Researchers at the University of British Columbia put Proverbs 16:24 to the test. They asked people who had high levels of anxiety to perform six random acts of kindness per week such as holding open doors, buying a friend's lunch, or donating to charity.

> Loving your neighbor doesn't have to be weird; it can actually make you cool!

Participants reported that after four weeks they felt less anxiety in general, more comfortable approaching people, and greater confidence in social interactions.[6] This works for neighbor kids, too: Middle school students who performed three kind acts a week for four weeks were happier and more popular at school—even though they did their kindnesses outside of school.[7]

God rewards our obedience to His command to be kind—

My child, never forget the things I have taught you. Store my commands in your heart. If you do this, you will live many years, and your life will be satisfying. *Never let loyalty and kindness leave you!* Tie them around your neck as a reminder. Write them deep within your heart. *Then you will find favor with both God and people, and you will earn a good reputation. . . .* Don't be impressed with your own wisdom. Instead, fear the Lord and turn away from evil. *Then you will have healing for your body and strength for your bones.*

Proverbs 3:1–4, 7–8 (emphasis added)

Loving your neighbor doesn't have to be weird; it can actually make you cool! Want God's favor on your life? Then obey His commands. Want other people to think well of you? Then treat them well. Be kind. Be faithful. Be merciful. Want to feel better? Try treating people better. Loving our neighbors because we love God is key to living the abundant life He promised.

## Eternal Impact

When we love our neighbors, we impact our local economy, the security of our community, and the health of our people. Because our relationships with our neighbors have eternal implications—for them and for us—God is right there to help with this exclusive guarantee:

> Feed the hungry, and help those in trouble. Then your light will shine out from the darkness, and the darkness around you will be as bright as noon. The Lord will guide you continually, giving you water when you are dry and restoring your strength. You will be like a well-watered garden, like an ever-flowing spring. Some of you will rebuild the deserted ruins of your cities. Then you will be known as a rebuilder of walls and a restorer of homes.
>
> Isaiah 58:10–12

God guarantees He will bless your humble offering of service to your neighbors. God guarantees He will magnify your effort and make you a light in your community. God guarantees He will guide you as you approach your neighbor's home. God guarantees He will strengthen and restore you if you feel spent, dry, used up, and parched as you care for His people. God guarantees you will earn a reputation not as the house with the biggest dandelions or the prettiest porch, but as the home where hope was found and hurting families experienced healing.

## Next Best Steps

1. Has your neighborhood ever been hit hard by a crisis? Have you seen beauty rise from the ashes of a fire, flood, tornado, hurricane, crime, or economic collapse?

2. What's the economic climate in your community? How has it impacted you personally? Has it affected your neighbors any differently?

3. How can you personally support your local economy? List stores, services, and civic issues you can support.

4. Have you been affected by a crime in your home? How do your neighbors look out for each other? What can you do to help neighbors get to know each other's names and be involved in your neighborhood?

5. Picture your most obnoxious neighbor, then pray a blessing over them. Post a reminder or set an alarm to pray this blessing for them three times a week.

6. What is your reputation in your neighborhood? Are you the grumpy neighbor or the fanatic? Are you the nice one? Maybe you're completely unknown. Think about what you would like to be known for in your neighborhood, and pray for this as you pray for your neighbor each day.

# Unwrapping Your Gifts

Her son was filthy. He was covered in dirt from head to toe, and grinning from ear to ear. A collection of rocks and flowers (aka weeds) was scattered on his blanket in the grass next to the community garden where his mother was working. That's when I knew I loved Lauren.

I love women who aren't afraid of a little dirt. When I found out Lauren was my neighbor, it was a bonus. But when I found out she had a burning desire to rake other people's leaves, it was an answered prayer. Lauren is a surgical technician in an endoscopy center, a career perfectly suited to her God-given gift for nurturing others. Since she wasn't meeting very many neighbors during colonoscopies, she emailed me her idea to start a neighborhood newsletter—something she had never done before. She wrote it and I made it look pretty, and together we passed it out door to door, pulling a cleaned-up Troy in his wagon behind us. The first issue featured Lauren's story about "Neighbors Helping Neighbors":

> As we all know, our neighborhood, like any other neighborhood, is full of needs. Some are seasonal, such as shoveling an elderly neighbor's driveway or raking leaves in the fall. Perhaps a neighbor has cancer and lives alone. I'm sure a medicine run or grocery run would lift his or her spirits! Perhaps you're my neighbor who just needs some extra help because of life in general.
>
> I am excited to say I am starting the Neighbors Helping Neighbors program intended just for those purposes! Now granted, I do not know exactly where to start, so here is my plan: If you are the person who needs a little extra help or companionship, or maybe you're a neighbor who would like to volunteer, or maybe you know your neighbor has a need and can direct me, please contact me. In the meanwhile you will probably see me in the neighborhood visiting door to door looking to offer my assistance.

Neighbors have helped neighbors, and Lauren's newsletter was the catalyst for our first Neighborhood Watch, block parties, community yard sales, and a baby shower. Every couple months, Lauren puts together a new issue, and neighbors use the Facebook page she created to volunteer to pass it out on their blocks. Lauren connects with our neighbors in multiple ways—online, in print, and in person—to accomplish her sole purpose: to meet the needs of the people living around her.

If Lauren filled out a questionnaire at church to reveal her spiritual gifts, her gift of mercy means she would quickly be tapped to visit people in the hospital or nursing home. With her gift of service, she could "do many tasks such as paint the walls, pick up trash, sort hymnals, clean the baptistry, keep the nursery or launder nursery bedding, cook meals, paint signs, drive the bus, help with the choir, run errands, serve as an audio-video worker, help with recordkeeping, be the church librarian, act as a greeter or an usher, serve as a stage hand in drama productions or as a photographer."[1] (And, of course, all young moms work in the nursery.)

These are all good, worthy, and important functions of any church. Spiritual gifts are foremost for the church and the kingdom. But since we spend about ninety minutes at church and around a hundred hours at home each week, let's explore ways to apply our spiritual gifts in very natural ways in our neighborhoods.

## What Is a Spiritual Gift?

Jesus wouldn't issue an impossible command to love our neighbor without equipping us to do so. God equips us to love our neighbor with spiritual gifts, which are the abilities given to each believer for the purpose of fulfilling His commands.

Believers have spiritual *attitudes* and spiritual *aptitudes*. Our spiritual *attitudes* are the *fruit* of the Spirit. They help us to act like Christ with love, joy, peace, patience, kindness, goodness, faithfulness, gentleness, and self-control (Galatians 5:22–23). Our spiritual *aptitudes* are the *function* of the Spirit; they are the spiritual gifts and supernatural strengths that make the church (and our neighborhoods) work.

There are three lists of spiritual gifts in the New Testament that use twenty different Greek words; they are found in

> Since we spend about ninety minutes at church and around a hundred hours at home each week, let's explore ways to apply our spiritual gifts in very natural ways in our neighborhoods.

1 Corinthians 12, Romans 12, and Ephesians 4. We'll explore how these gifts operate in the church and in our neighborhoods. In alphabetical order, the gifts are:

**Administration**—The ability to plan, organize, supervise, and direct people toward the accomplishment of goals. A person with this gift probably has a color-coded calendar synchronized between her computer and smartphone. She puts things on her to-do list for the sheer thrill of checking them off. Sometimes her own list overwhelms her, but she knows how to manage her time, prioritize her work, and build a team. If you purged, organized, and labeled the crayons, prizes, and snacks in the preschool classroom at church, you might have this gift. If you have the urge to organize the Neighborhood Watch, create a neighborhood directory, or plan a block party, this may be your gift.

**Apostle**—Someone who leads churches and has spiritual authority. If you're an apostle, you may have people serving under you to help accomplish your hopes, dreams, and vision for the church. At home, your neighbors could easily catch your vision and be eager to help build a sense of community.

**Discernment**—The ability to distinguish truth and lies. Discerning people are quick to spot a scam, are very clear on doctrine, and can help point out spiritual attacks or lies of the enemy. If you have the gift of discernment, you may see things others don't—as a result, people may not believe you or you may be misunderstood often. At church, the gift of discernment can help you sense others' motives, point out when someone is trying to tear apart a team, and recognize when sermons don't line up with Scripture. At home, you know when a well-kept lawn hides an unkempt family that is falling apart, and your hackles go up when crime is afoot.

**Evangelism**—The fervent desire to share the Good News of the Gospel. Evangelists lead people to Christ on airplanes and in line at the grocery store. Bible verses ooze out of the person with this gift, and they carry tracts in their car. At church, a person with this gift is drawn to the outreach team, leading mission trips to the far corners of the earth and right around the corner. At home, they will invite the neighbor children for an Easter egg hunt or Christmas cookie decorating party—and then explain why we celebrate these holidays.

**Exhortation**—Your friends know they've got a friend in you. This Greek word for exhortation, *parakaleō*, means "to call to one's side." This is the person who comes running with encouragement, comfort, consolation, and counsel when anyone calls. At church, their practical teaching and patient advice help people become mature Christians. At home, they're the one neighbors seek for comfort for everything from burnt dinners to overdoses.

**Faith**—Utter conviction about God's power and promises that is unshaken by circumstances or obstacles. A person with the gift of faith is a prayer warrior who is happily dependent on God. They take big risks, expecting God to show up and show off. If you are drawn to your church's prayer ministry and the mission field, you might have this gift. At home, nothing deters this person's hope and hard work to see salvation for their neighbors.

**Giving**—The ability to share your material resources cheerfully and without thinking of how you're going to be repaid. This gift is measured by the size of your heart, not your wallet—although this person does enjoy making significant financial gifts. A person with this gift helps with benevolence and missions and gives of their time and talent as well as their funds (often anonymously). At home, they give neighbors plants from their garden and food from their kitchen. They feel blessed to share what they have been given.

**Healing**—To be used by God to make others whole either physically, emotionally, mentally, or spiritually. Healers are a conduit for God's power. At church, you may feel the pull to regularly pray with and for others; counseling and recovery ministries are close to your heart. If your heart breaks for the suffering you see around your home, and you often pray specifically over neighbors' homes, you may have this gift. You will be drawn to those who are hurting in mind, body, or spirit.

**Helps**—A helper gives support or assistance that frees others for ministry. You have to look hard for this person, because they happily hide in the wings and behind the scenes at church—yet they're indispensable to those with more recognizable faces. At home, they baby-sit the neighbor's children, plus they'll feed the cat and water your flowers while you're on vacation.

**Knowledge**—An intelligence and understanding of Christianity. A person with this gift is a fact-gatherer, an analyzer, an information storehouse. They love learning, research, and investigation. You may find yourself lending your knowledge (and your library!) to others; you're a storehouse of trivia. At church you want to lead in-depth Bible studies; at home, you're the one to call when your neighbors need a bit of local history or zoning laws.

**Leadership**—The ability to manage and motivate others to get involved. Leaders have high expectations that can either push others to greater heights or make them want to jump off a cliff. Leaders constantly come up with new ideas. At church, leaders may easily see ways to improve existing programs or develop new ones. At home, they initiate neighborhood safety watches, Homeowner's Associations, and holiday celebrations.

**Mercy**—Sensitivity and sympathy toward those who are suffering. People with the gift of mercy are *moved* with compassion; they take action to alleviate other people's pain. You can't just watch infomercials about starving children on television; you want to go to Africa. At church, you long to embrace the lost and unlovable. At home, you'll knock on a battered door to reach the battered woman inside.

**Miracles**—To be enabled by God with strength, power, and ability to perform supernatural feats that result in praise to God. At church, a person with the gift of miracles is usually somewhere in the picture when amazing, inexplicable things happen. At home, you want to see mountains move as neighbors' lives are transformed.

**Pastor**—A shepherd who finds and saves lost sheep, then loves them, patches their wounds, shares their lives, and keeps watch for predators. Pastorally gifted people can pastor a small group or ministry team; they care deeply about others' needs and growth. In the neighborhood, they're on the lookout for the lonely, the lost, and the just plain stubborn.

**Prophecy**—Hearing from God and speaking to people. God puts His words in a prophet's mouth, so these words always line up perfectly with Scripture. A prophet's words don't always make you feel all warm and fuzzy inside, because they can expose the secrets of the heart (1 Corinthians 14:25), but in the end these words always strengthen, encourage, and comfort (1 Corinthians 14:3). A person with a prophetic gift has the perfect verse on the tip of their tongue to help someone at church, and at home they are able to apply Scripture to everyday circumstances.

**Service**—The gift of knowing what needs to be done and doing it without being asked. This is the gift you want your children to have. This person doesn't ask if the garbage needs to be taken out, they simply see the overflowing trash can and take care of it. At church, they're task-oriented and capable of getting more done in a day than most do in a month. At home, they lend a hand, an ear, or a shoulder whenever neighbors need it.

**Teaching**—The ability to clearly explain and instruct others. A teacher takes complicated material and makes it seem simple. At church, a teacher's ability results in understanding, application, and maturity—not just intellectual stimulation. At home, she's a Titus 2 woman (and she actually knows what that means) who teaches her neighbors how to love their families and care for their homes.

**Tongues**—The ability to speak in a language not previously learned so unbelievers can hear God's message in their own language or the body can be edified. Tongues is related to **Interpretation of Tongues**—The ability to translate the message of someone who has spoken in tongues. At church, 1 Corinthians 14:6 says the gift of tongues and interpretation should bring "revelation or some special knowledge or prophecy or teaching." At home, the gift of tongues could help you communicate with neighbors who speak a different language, either literally or figuratively. Whether or not your personal understanding of spiritual gifts includes the present-day usage of the gift of tongues, we can all agree that we need a God-given ability to communicate with people who don't share our vocabulary or worldview.

**Wisdom**—The ability to apply spiritual knowledge in practical ways in everyday life. A wise person is circumspect, seeing all sides of a situation, including extenuating circumstances and potential consequences. They're known for street smarts and common sense. At church, you understand how to apply

Scripture in context. At home, you get the desperate middle-of-the-night calls for advice.

This isn't an all-inclusive list, and there are other spiritual gifts mentioned outside of these passages, such as:

- **Celibacy**—The ability to remain single without regret so you can serve the Lord without distraction.
- **Hospitality**—To put people at ease by warmly welcoming them into your home or church (much more on this in chapter 9!).
- **Martyrdom**—To give your life for the cause of Christ.
- **Missionary**—To be a servant of the Gospel in another culture (which can be right next door).
- **Voluntary Poverty**—To purposely give all your material resources to help others.

There are also skills that can have the impact of a spiritual gift:

- **Craftsmanship**—Exodus 35 refers to "artisans called by God" to help build the tabernacle who are filled "with the Spirit of God, in wisdom and understanding, in knowledge and all manner of workmanship, to design artistic works . . ." In your neighborhood, your gift of craftsmanship could be used to beautify homes and public spaces or simply help a neighbor complete a project.
- **Music**—The ability to play musical instruments and sing can be used to glorify God. At church, "Sing hymns instead of drinking songs! Sing songs from your heart to Christ. Sing praises over everything . . ." (Ephesians 5:18–19 THE MESSAGE) and praise the Lord with a full orchestra of musical instruments (Psalm 150). At home, playing oldies, holiday favorites, and secular songs with clean lyrics are fun ways to bond.
- **Writing**—Beautiful words can stir hearts (Psalm 45:1). Both John and Paul wrote about the act of writing as

a way to encourage and instruct the church. At home, a written note or handwritten card will stay on your neighbor's fridge long after it's been delivered, and a simple text, email, or Facebook post can leave a lasting impression.

## Unwrapping Your Gifts

My husband is known for choosing thoughtful gifts as well as creative adventures in gift wrapping—it's impossible to guess what's inside his lumpy, bumpy packages. One Christmas, he and our daughter rolled out an antique shopping cart loaded with crazily wrapped presents. The cart is amazing; I use it every day in our laundry room. Inside were lovely gifts like a skillet I needed, and a cute purse, too.

Taking another package from the cart, I could clearly feel a spray pump and I wondered what it could be—perfume? Body spray? Well, it *was* scented . . . it was a bottle of French lavender multipurpose cleaner. This was followed by almond floor cleaner and three or four other "gourmet" cleaning products, but my favorite was the teardrop-shaped bottle of eucalyptus mint toilet bowl cleaner.

David giggled but I was annoyed. "How many women get toilet bowl cleaner for Christmas?" he laughed.

"Not very many—I hope!" I replied through clenched teeth.

He had even wrapped a duster and a bucket—yes, he wrapped a bucket. "Remember the purse. Look at the shopping cart. Don't hit him with the frying pan," I told myself. After I had unwrapped the entire cleaning aisle, David pulled out one last gift—a tube with tassels on each end. In keeping with the theme, I was not surprised to unwrap an empty paper towel tube—but I was very surprised by what I found tucked inside: a gift certificate for a housekeeping service!

Now, *that's* what I'm talking about! That's a good gift!

So if you sinful people know how to give good gifts to your children, how much more will your heavenly Father give good gifts to those who ask him.

Matthew 7:11

The first gift we receive from our heavenly Father is the gift of salvation through Jesus Christ, who stepped down from heaven to deliver that gift on the first Christmas morning. We receive the gift of the Holy Spirit, and the gift of eternal life. But God, because of His generous and abundant grace, doesn't stop there! He pours spiritual gifts on us like Santa with his bottomless bag of goodies.

At first, I didn't think the toilet bowl cleaner wrapped up under my Christmas tree would be part of such a good gift. Sometimes spiritual gifts take a little bit of patience to unwrap too.

**Sometimes spiritual gifts come wrapped in a problem.** You may never know what you're capable of until there's a crisis, a demand you can't meet on your own power. When we seek the giver, His grace will supply the gifts needed for every situation.

**Sometimes spiritual gifts come wrapped in a compliment.** Don't shrug it off when someone pays you a compliment. God often uses the insight of other people to help us figure out what we're good at.

**Sometimes spiritual gifts come wrapped in a paycheck.** You may have developed skills and abilities at work that God would very much like you to use at church and at home. Likewise, take your ministry talents to work and unwrap them on the job! You'll be blessed when you find fulfilling, energizing ways to use your God-given gifts at work. Your employer will be blessed when they get supernatural abilities for the same wage, and the kingdom of God will be blessed when co-workers see your Christlike attitude as you perform your everyday job.

**Sometimes spiritual gifts come wrapped in a request.** If you're asked to do something beyond your comfort zone, don't automatically say no. Your unique gifts might just be the answer to someone's prayers. Pray about it yourself, and see if God is preparing a new gift for you.

**Sometimes spiritual gifts come wrapped in a passion.** Paul said in 1 Corinthians 9:16, "Woe is me if I do not preach the gospel!" (NKJV). Teaching and evangelism were Paul's gifts, and he felt the weight of them. What passion do you carry like a heavy package that you are compelled to open and use?

Your gifts are given *to you* but they are *for others.*

A spiritual gift is given to each of us so we can *help each other.*

1 Corinthians 12:7 (emphasis added)

God has given each of you a gift from his great variety of spiritual gifts. Use them well to *serve one another.*

1 Peter 4:10 (emphasis added)

Now these are the gifts Christ gave to the church: the apostles, the prophets, the evangelists, and the pastors and teachers. Their responsibility is to equip God's people to *do his work* and build up the church, the body of Christ.

Ephesians 4:11–12 (emphasis added)

## What Will You Do With Your Gift?

Your spiritual gifts are God's supernatural power working its way through your words, your works, and your walk to take His witness to the world. You don't have to have a title or position to use your spiritual gifts, and there's no age restriction. The gifts are not commands, and they are not constant. They work in combination and they increase with exercise. All of our gifts work together inside the church to reach those who are outside. What will you do with your gift?

**You can return your gift.** Have you ever witnessed the embarrassing scene when a child receives a gift and ungratefully tosses it aside? That's what Zechariah did when an angel told him his way-too-old-to-have-a-baby wife, Elizabeth, was going to have a son. He responded, "Do you expect me to believe this?" (Luke 1:18 THE MESSAGE). You, too, can refuse to believe God would give you such an important gift and can reject or return it.

> Your gifts are given to you but they are for others.

**You can accept your gift.** Mary answered differently when the same angel told her she would conceive the Christ child. "I am the Lord's servant. May everything you have said about me come true" (Luke 1:38). Mary's humble response said, "I don't understand how you're going to do this, Lord, and I don't know why you chose me—but I'm willing to be used for your glory."

**You can exchange your gift.** You can exchange your gift if you don't like it. Never mind that your gift was chosen for God's glory, go ahead and swap it for something that fits a little more comfortably. The instructions are in Romans 1:25:

> They traded the truth about God for a lie. So they worshiped and served the things God created instead of the Creator himself, who is worthy of eternal praise! Amen.
>
> Romans 1:25

**You can ignore your gift.** You can put your gift on a shelf and never touch it. Beware if you do this, because God uses gifts of the Holy Spirit to confirm the message of salvation (Hebrews 2:1–4). If you ignore your gifts, you're in danger of drifting away from His touch. Ignoring your spiritual gifts makes you wither away, harms the church, and could rob others of the chance to experience salvation.

**You can use your gift.** Use your gifts to do something to meet another's needs. Show your faith—and your love, and your appreciation—by using your God-given gifts to do good to others.

## I'll Brew the Beans If You'll Bring a Mug

The first time I had an Open House in my neighborhood, I invited eighty-nine women. (It's a big neighborhood, and I have a big family room.) If they all came, I was worried I'd run out of coffee mugs—so at the last minute I added this line to the invitation: *I'll brew the beans if you'll bring a mug.* I've kept that line on every invitation because it turned out to be a powerful lesson: Bringing her own mug made each woman a participant instead of an observer. Women I had never met showed up at my door clutching their mugs to their chests! Each mug was a conversation starter, an instant icebreaker. It gave her something to do, a task to perform, a role to fulfill.

Women want to be useful. We want to participate, not be bystanders. We crave accomplishment and a sense that we've done something purposeful and permanent. Working together with our neighbors gives all of us a chance to find fulfillment using our untapped, unwrapped gifts. In my neighborhood, we progressed from simply bringing a mug to a meeting, to having a baby shower for one of our neighbors. We took meals to funeral dinners and donated a portion of our community yard sale profits to a diaper drive. We planned a neighborhood block party and started a Neighborhood Watch, and now we're working together on developing a neighborhood park.

## Use It or Lose It

It's nice to be on the receiving end of a good gift, isn't it? It's also fun to give gifts—as every Black Friday shopper fighting crowds at

3:00 a.m. understands! Why do we *do* that? Why do we make shopping lists, scour the ads, go out in the cold, and fight the crowds?

Sure, we all want to save a little money, and some people—you know who you are—actually *enjoy* shopping. But what really motivates us is the look on our loved one's face the moment they open that package and find the perfect gift tucked inside, and the joy we know they'll receive from our gift for a long time to come.

Tucked inside each of us is a very special spiritual gift from our heavenly Father. He spared no expense to bring this gift to you; He paid for it with the precious blood of His only Son. He waits for the perfect moment to present His gift to you, and then I think He sits back with a knowing smile as He watches you unwrap the treasures He's chosen especially for you. He knows what gift you need before you even ask, and He knows exactly what your neighbors need, too.

> **Women want to be useful. We want to participate, not be bystanders. We crave accomplishment and a sense that we've done something purposeful and permanent.**

# Next Best Steps

1. Circle the gifts that resonate with you or make your heart beat a little bit faster. Or, if someone comes to mind, write their name beside their gift.

2. What does your church do to reach those outside the church? What do you do personally to reach people outside the church?

3. Take an online quiz to help you unwrap your spiritual gifts, ask your church leaders if they administer or recommend a particular test, or ask a close friend to help identify your gifts.

4. How are you using your gifts at church? At work? At home?

5. What is your, "Woe is me if I do not _____!"? Fill in the blank with a passion God has planted in your soul. Don't hyper-spiritualize your response: your woe can be a very practical calling like quilting, making cakes, writing poems, fixing cars, or playing sports.

6. How can your spiritual gifts be used very practically and naturally to love your neighbor? Make a list that matches your gift(s) to a very specific neighbor's need. What is the next best step you need to put this gift to use?

7. What projects could you work on together with your neighbors to utilize each person's spiritual gifts?

# Say What?

The glittery snowflake ornaments I had purchased for the neighbors on my street, a cheery greeting tied to each one, were getting tangled in a bag in my car—and it was the morning of Christmas Eve. "It's now or never," I scolded myself, so I washed my face and put on a hat to cover my messy bedhead, then set out to wish my neighbors a merry Christmas.

No one answered at the first two houses, so I hung the ornament on their doorknobs and moved on. The neighbors who were home seemed delighted and we quickly exchanged holiday pleasantries. At the last house, however, a man I barely knew swung the door wide open and invited me inside. "Tina, we have a visitor!" he called to his wife.

Tom and Tina lived just two houses up from me, but I had only met them twice in the past twelve years. When I invited her to an Open House several years before, she explained that she worked full time. We waved if we happened to catch each other outside, and they came to our neighborhood block party a few months before. Otherwise, the yards that separated us might as well have been miles.

Tom ushered me into their delicious-smelling kitchen and pulled out a barstool at the island. Every burner was bubbling with something wonderful, the oven was full, and several Crock-Pots lined the counters. Tina came around a corner pulling her robe tightly closed and gave me a friendly but awkward smile—poor thing, her husband had invited the crazy neighbor lady in while she was still wearing her pajamas, on Christmas Eve of all days!

> The yards that separated us might as well have been miles.

This is a turning point in any tenuous neighborly relationship, and Tina turned it in a new and beautiful direction when she asked, "Would you like a meatball?" In the midst of a busy holiday—and getting ready for their son's wedding just three days later!—my neighbors welcomed me, fed me, and became my friends. (Tom and Tina, I should probably warn you that meatballs for breakfast at your house is my new Christmas Eve tradition. I'll be over around ten!)

Depending on your personality, approaching your neighbor might not bother you in the least. Or the thought of knocking on your neighbor's door might make you weak in the knees! Both reactions are completely normal. What can you expect when you meet your neighbor? What should you say? What might they say? Thankfully, Jesus himself gave us some very helpful advice as He sent His disciples to do the very same thing I am asking of you.

They were travelling through the region of Galilee, where Jesus had grown up, passing through towns and villages not unlike your very own neighborhood. Jesus was disturbed by what He saw: "When he saw the crowds, he had compassion on them because they were confused and helpless, like sheep without a shepherd" (Matthew 9:36).

I have to tell you that television commercials can move me with compassion—returning soldiers surprising their momma with a cup of coffee on Christmas morning, sad-faced puppies abandoned on the side of the road, hungry babies languishing in their mothers' arms. But unlike Jesus, I'm rarely moved with compassion just walking down my street. The Greek word for compassion in this passage is *splagchnizomai,* and it is a gut-wrenching, heart-turning, feet-moving kind of pity that is only used of Jesus. "The original word is a very remarkable one," said noted nineteenth-century preacher Charles Spurgeon. "It is not found in classic Greek. It is not found in the Septuagint [the Greek version of the Old Testament]. The fact is, it was a word coined by the evangelists themselves. They did not find one in the whole Greek language that suited their purpose, and therefore they had to make one."[1]

While others may have seen farmers and fishermen, Jesus saw people who were harassed and helpless, confused and aimless. He saw the weariness in their bones, their exhaustion and hopelessness, their anxiety and fear. He saw that they had been discarded by society, tossed aside and ignored. He saw that they were unprotected, unloved, uncared for. He saw they had no one looking out for them, no one tending to their needs, no one sharing their joys and sorrows.

> **Then Jesus stopped praying and did something about it.**

This isn't a first-century problem or a third-world problem. Every day on every street—in your neighborhood—people feel abandoned and alone. In their desperate search for fulfillment they sample every conceivable distraction—toys, entertainment, alcohol, drugs, shopping, acquisition, avoidance. In their longing for love, they give away their bodies and their souls. In their quest for safety, they arm themselves with worldly weapons—big guns, strong arms, and loud words meant to intimidate and alienate.

Jesus was so moved with compassion for these people, His neighbors, that He asked His followers to pray that the Lord would send someone to help them.

> He said to his disciples, "The harvest is great, but the workers are few. So pray to the Lord who is in charge of the harvest; ask him to send more workers into his fields."
>
> Matthew 9:37–38

Then Jesus stopped praying and did something about it.

## Do Something

Jesus called His twelve closest disciples together and said, "You—yeah, you. You are the ones I'm sending out to love your neighbor. Let me show you how." This is still our command today. Let's use modern language for our modern assignment by studying Matthew 10 in *The Message*:

> The prayer was no sooner prayed than it was answered. Jesus called twelve of his followers and sent them into the ripe fields. He gave them power to kick out the evil spirits and to tenderly care for the bruised and hurt lives.
>
> Matthew 10:1 THE MESSAGE

Jesus' request for workers in the harvest fields wasn't a far-off, maybe-someday kind of prayer. It was a right-now, right-here prayer, and the answers were sitting right in front of Him.

> This is the list of the twelve he sent: Simon (they called him Peter, or "Rock"); Andrew, his brother; James, Zebedee's son; John, his brother; Philip; Bartholomew; Thomas; Matthew, the tax

man; James, son of Alphaeus; Thaddaeus; Simon, the Canaanite; Judas Iscariot (who later turned on him).

*Matthew 10:2–4 THE MESSAGE*

When you pray for your neighbors, you just might be the answer you are looking for! Don't be surprised if God doesn't answer your prayers with an army of angels. He has already sent *you*, His healer and harvester, into a neighborhood ripe for salvation. God works through crises, catastrophes, and common people just like us.

> **When you pray for your neighbors, you just might be the answer you are looking for!**

Jesus sent his twelve harvest hands out with this charge: "Don't begin by traveling to some far-off place to convert unbelievers. And don't try to be dramatic by tackling some public enemy."

*Matthew 10:5 THE MESSAGE*

Most of us will have neither the time, money, nor inclination to go to a foreign country to spread the Gospel, but this does not excuse us from our missionary calling in our own backyard. Jesus would later tell His disciples to go into all the world, but initially He told them to start close to home. He never lost sight of their literal next-door neighbors. He knew that day-to-day drama was more important to their neighbors than international headlines.

Go to the lost, confused people right here in the neighborhood. Tell them that the kingdom is here. Bring health to the sick. Raise the dead. Touch the untouchables. Kick out the demons.

*Matthew 10:6–8 THE MESSAGE*

There's plenty of work to be done at home. Sometimes we become distracted with religious mathematics that measure Sunday morning attendance, the number of ladies at our last tea, or the weekly offering. These are important statistics: Every tick mark represents a soul; every dollar represents a good deed the church can do. But what if we measured the success of our churches by the number of women who visit abortion clinics? What if we based our success on pornography sales, suicide rates, drug use, teen pregnancy, divorce, prison population, graduation rate, poverty level, and unemployment? There are sick people living on our streets, walking dead in our malls, untouchables in our grocery aisles, demons prowling our schools. What would our community look like if we measured the success of our churches by the health of our neighborhoods?

> **What would our community look like if we measured the success of our churches by the health of our neighborhoods?**

> You have been treated generously, so live generously.
>
> Matthew 10:8 THE MESSAGE

When I think of all Jesus has done for me, I'm embarrassed by how little I do for others. If my life was truly a tribute to His generosity, I would never tire of loving my neighbors. But the truth is, I do. Whether I'm weary, worried, or obstinate, this reminder pulls me from the couch to the street.

> Don't think you have to put on a fund-raising campaign before you start. You don't need a lot of equipment. You are the equipment, and all you need to keep that going is three meals a day. Travel light.
>
> Matthew 10:9–10 THE MESSAGE

Loving our neighbor doesn't have to be a big production. We don't have to throw fancy parties or elaborate events. Inviting one woman over for a glass of sweet tea on the front porch is all that's necessary. We don't need training courses or evangelism workshops—truth be told, you don't really even need this book. *You* are all you need—your personality, your strengths, even your weaknesses are God's perfect plan for your particular neighborhood. Don't stress over it, enjoy it. God will give you everything you need to do what He asks.

> When you enter a town or village, don't insist on staying in a luxury inn. Get a modest place with some modest people, and be content there until you leave.
>
> Matthew 10:11 THE MESSAGE

Being content in our neighborhoods means being patient, determined, and persistent. Aristotle said, "The desire for friendship comes quickly; friendship does not." Modest folks in modest homes are of great value to God, and He smiles at our modest moves toward friendship. My vision for neighborhood friendships looked a lot like the classic 1971 Coca-Cola commercial: "I'd like to teach the world to sing in perfect harmony. I'd like to buy the world a Coke, and keep it company." Jesus reminds me to set aside my grand delusions and be content with simple gestures.

> **You** are all you need—your personality, your strengths, even your weaknesses are God's perfect plan for your particular neighborhood.

> When you knock on a door, be courteous in your greeting.
>
> Matthew 10:12 THE MESSAGE

Knock. Smile. Speak. It's that simple! Not much has changed from Jesus' Israeli neighborhoods to wherever you live today. Do you think Jesus foresaw me, little ol' me, knocking on my neighbor's door when He gave this instruction? Did He picture each door in your neighborhood? Did He know the exact moment you would raise your hand to knock, and prepare the hearts inside to receive your greeting?

> If they welcome you, be gentle in your conversation.
>
> Matthew 10:13 THE MESSAGE

I'm usually so wrapped up in my own anxiety when I knock on a neighbor's door that I forget this is all about *them*. Pay attention to how long it takes them to answer the door. They may be busy, sleeping, working, or in the middle of their favorite movie. Pay attention to their body language and the words they say—and what goes unsaid. Be considerate, gentle, and kind. If they are open to you, be open to them.

> When you step foot off your front porch, you have officially entered Satan's battleground.

> If they don't welcome you, quietly withdraw. Don't make a scene. Shrug your shoulders and be on your way.
>
> Matthew 10:14 THE MESSAGE

Trust me, you will know if your neighbor is not interested in making your acquaintance. They may barely crack open the screen door; they may not open the door at all, even if you can see them inside. They may be as nervous about answering the door as you were about knocking! I don't like to answer my phone if the Caller ID doesn't tell me who it is, let alone answer my door when a stranger knocks. Be sensitive to your neighbor's reaction. If she takes a step back, you take a step back. Mirror her reaction. Don't be weird by being pushy.

> You can be sure that on Judgment Day they'll be mighty sorry—but it's no concern of yours now.
>
> Matthew 10:15 THE MESSAGE

You know what? This is a big deal, with big consequences. Your first conversation with a neighbor could lead to a friendship. That friendship could lead to the opportunity to tell them about Jesus Christ. However, their reaction is not your responsibility. Jesus will handle eternity; you just think about today.

> Stay alert. This is hazardous work I'm assigning you. You're going to be like sheep running through a wolf pack, so don't call attention to yourselves. Be as cunning as a snake, inoffensive as a dove.
>
> Matthew 10:16 THE MESSAGE

When you step foot off your front porch, you have officially entered Satan's battleground. Be armed with prayer, and be aware of the warfare around you. You want to be remembered for your kindness, not causing contention. Leave a good impression. You are not in your neighborhood to prove a point or win a battle; you are there out of submission and obedience to Christ.

> Don't be naive. Some people will impugn your motives, others will smear your reputation—just because you believe in me. Don't be upset when they haul you before the civil authorities. Without knowing it, they've done you—and me—a favor, given you a platform for preaching the kingdom news!
>
> Matthew 10:17–18 THE MESSAGE

When you speak for Christ, some people will speak against you. Expect it. Things might get sticky, but your job is to live in such a way that no one can say anything bad about you (1 Peter 2:12).

> And don't worry about what you'll say or how you'll say it. The right words will be there; the Spirit of your Father will supply the words.
>
> Matthew 10:19–20 THE MESSAGE

There's only so much you can script and rehearse when you step out in your neighborhood. This may be one of the biggest leaps of faith you'll ever take, and it's a chance to learn as much about God as your neighbors. You can trust Him to tell you what to say and how to say it, just like He did for Jesus (John 12:49).

## A Gift in Hand

Do you like raisins? How about figs? Me neither. But we can learn something about loving our neighbors from these sticky (I would say "icky") dried fruits.

Raisin cakes were a common food in Bible times. I have no idea what raisin cakes are, and I have no interest in mixing up a batch (although that hard clump of raisins in my cupboard may qualify). Here's what I do know: everyone loves free food. Women of the Bible knew this and used it to their advantage.

> It's easier to knock on your neighbor's door with one hand when you're holding a gift in the other.

Take Abigail, for example. Abigail was in big trouble with her neighbors (1 Samuel 25). This smart and sassy woman lost no time preparing raisin cakes and other delicacies to appease an invading tribe. Her gift was accepted and her neighborhood was saved. Abigail's thoughtful and generous gift made her neighbor stop long enough to listen to her humble and gracious words.

Queen Esther knew this too. She prepared a lavish banquet for King Xerxes to soften his heart when she asked him a big favor (Esther 5). In fact, she invited him to dinner twice before she asked him to have mercy on her neighbors (Esther 7:1–4).

These women demonstrated a principle that's plainly spelled out for us in one simple verse: "Giving a gift can open doors; it gives access to important people!" (Proverbs 18:16).

146

It's easier to knock on your neighbor's door with one hand when you're holding a gift in the other. Having a gift in hand to present to your neighbors gives you something to talk about as soon as the door is opened. Please don't clutch your pocketbook when I mention giving a gift to everyone in your neighborhood. This can be simple, adorable, and affordable. The sparkly snowflakes I passed out on my street at Christmas cost about a quarter apiece, bought in bulk at a local craft store with a coupon.

Here are some modest gifts you can prepare for your neighbors:

- Individual packet of instant coffee or water flavoring mix (such as Starbucks VIA or Crystal Light)
- Keurig cup
- Tea bag
- Cocoa mix
- Hard candy
- Snack-sized portion of cookies or chips
- Seed packet
- Artificial flower stem
- Children's drawing
- Greeting card
- Holiday themes: Valentine card, Easter egg, American flag, Christmas ornament

If you're giving food to people you've never met, I recommend it be factory sealed. Frankly, I would not eat a homemade food gift from someone if I've never seen their kitchen, so save your special recipes for neighbors who are already friends. It's easy to place several small wrapped candies in a clear storage bag or decorative cello bag (found in the craft or gift section) and tie it with curling ribbon. Use a long piece of ribbon, about 24 inches, tied into a bow with big loops so you can hang your gift with a note on a doorknob if no one is home.

## What to Say

Come on, let's go talk to your neighbors! You've prayed with every step. Now you're ready to ring your first doorbell.

As the door chimes, you and your neighbor both take a big gulp. "Hello?" she asks. It's a question. She means, "Who are you? What do you want? Why are you here?"

> "My name is Amy and I live right over there (pointing), on the corner of Rosewood and Longwood Drive. I wanted to introduce myself and give this to you."

If a man answers the door, I immediately ask if his wife or the "lady of the house" is home; I never go inside unless there's another woman present. I always tell my neighbors who I am and where I live, to let them know I'm a neighbor and not a salesperson or a con artist. This is also where the little gift comes in really handy!

> "I've lived here for several years, but it's been hard to get to know the people living right around me. I finally realized it wasn't going to happen unless I did something about it, so I'm introducing myself to my neighbors. May I ask your name?"

This is when you may have to swallow your pride and admit you don't know your neighbor's name, even if you've been casually chatting with them for years. This is embarrassing, no doubt about it—and important. Dale Carnegie said, "A person's name is to him or her the sweetest and most important sound in any language." Try this:

> "I'm so sorry. I should know your name but I don't recall. Could you tell me your name again?"

Repeat their name and use it in your conversation as often as you can without sounding unnatural. If it's an unusual name or one that could be spelled several ways, ask them to spell it—this also helps burn their name in your brain. Use their name when you say good-bye, and repeat your own name so they don't feel awkward.

Here are two different reactions you might receive:

1. A warm smile as she opens the door wide. If this happens, elaborate on what you're doing and why; ask if she knows any of your other neighbors.
2. A guarded expression and barely outstretched hand. In this case, be brief. Don't make her feel uncomfortable or threatened. Let her end the conversation when she wants. Don't allow yourself to become frustrated or discouraged.

Most of the women I've met have expressed the same sentiment: They want to know their neighbors, but they don't know how. Most of the time, this is the launch for a friendly conversation as we talk about how long we've lived here, who we know in common, and what we love about our neighborhood. We've talked about pets and vacations and schools and gardening and food and kids—conversations we never would have had if I hadn't knocked on their door.

If you're hosting an Open House, block party, wine tasting, book club, or other event, this is the perfect time to extend your invitation.

**"I'm having an [insert your event here] on [insert date here].
Are you free on Fridays?"**

It's not likely your neighbor will answer your invitation immediately unless she knows she is unavailable, and that's fine. This question doesn't put her on the spot. If she knows she's unavailable, ask if another day or time would work better for her in case you have another event. Invite her to come anytime or to stop by the next time she's taking a walk.

Since I also host a Neighborhood Café Bible study after my Open House, I always mention it. I don't ever want my neighbors to feel that I've pulled a bait-and-switch tactic to trick them into Bible study. I usually say something like this—

> "After the Open House, we're going to continue to get together every other Friday morning. We'll always have some good food to share, and I'll read a devotional after we spend some time getting to know each other. The dates are on the back of your invitation."

This is met with either excitement or indifference. Women who never go to church have embraced the idea, and faithful churchgoers have said, "That's just not my thing." Their response is not my responsibility, I remind myself. Sometimes a woman will reply, "I already have a church," in which case I assure her that a neighborhood Bible study unites women from many different churches; I also let her know all women in the neighborhood are invited regardless of where they attend church—even if they don't attend church at all.

**Their response is not my responsibility.**

> "Even if you aren't able or interested in the devotional, I do hope you'll come to the Open House just to say hello and meet some of our neighbors. I'm inviting everyone on our street."

I want my neighbors to know that the Open House is for everyone, even if they have no intent or desire to come to the Bible study.

I carry a notebook with me to immediately write down new names and any tidbits I learn about my neighbors. You could also use your smartphone to make a voice recording or text memo, or even send yourself an email.

## Fill It Up

Inviting your neighbors into your home, into your life, is a test and a testimony. Jesus told a parable about a man who prepared a great feast and sent out many invitations. The man told his servant, "Go out into the country lanes and behind the hedges and urge anyone you find to come, so that the house will be full" (Luke 14:23).

It's time to fill your house, so that He can fill His.

# Next Best Steps

1. How do you try to "live properly among your unbelieving neighbors," as it says in 1 Peter 2:12? Have you ever been falsely accused by a neighbor? Have you ever been vindicated by your reputation and actions?

2. What scares you about having the first conversation with a neighbor you've never met before? Read John 12:49. Have you ever felt that God showed you what to say and how to say it?

3. Write a sample script you will use as a starting point. Rehearse it. Smile while you say it. Now tear it up and say a prayer that God will give you words to speak.

4. Read the story of how Abigail saved her neighborhood in 1 Samuel 25. Do you have a "Nabal" in your neighborhood who endangers others? Have you ever appeased someone—or been appeased yourself—by a gift or kind gesture?

5. Have you ever been honored by an invitation to someone's home? How did Esther's invitation to the king in Esther 5 and 7 affect their relationship?

6. Circle a date on your calendar when you will knock on one neighbor's door to introduce yourself. Tell one friend about your commitment and ask them to hold you accountable.

# Martha Unleashed

We lived in utopia. Our Disneyesque neighborhood was designed for community from the ground up with welcoming front porches and wide sidewalks. Our brand-new foursquare looked like a centuries-old farmhouse. It was on the same street as the model homes, so we were provided with a "Private Residence" sign to keep homebuyers from wandering into our living room. We lived across the street from a park with a playground and hiking trails; down the block from the pool and community center; and a short walk away from our own library and elementary school, a YMCA, restaurants and shops, and even our own Starbucks—the only thing missing was a white steepled church. Our full-time activities director arranged carriage rides at Christmas and bicycle parades on the Fourth of July. The neighborhood attracted people who wanted to be neighborly, and we made friends quickly and easily.

After living in a dream house in a dreamy neighborhood, it's no surprise we had a hard time finding a new home when we moved several states away. I stayed down south with a toddler and a dog and tried to sell one house, while David worked up north and tried to find a new one. After months of fruitless house hunting, he called one day with a prospect. When I asked him to describe it (this was way back in the days before smartphones and real estate websites), he replied, "It's really *ugly*." When I asked him to tell me something good about it, he said, "It's really *big*."

Do you know what that house was? A really big, ugly house. I could barely sign the contract through my tears. It was dreadfully ugly! It was dated and dingy and dark. Unoccupied for nearly two years, it was overgrown and uncared for. Our daughter wasn't allowed off the sidewalk because of the poison ivy infestation. It smelled bad.

On moving day, the septic system didn't work. Our refrigerator didn't fit in the kitchen, but my husband managed to find his circular saw on the moving truck and cut off a few inches of countertop—after he ripped down a cabinet and ripped off the suspended ceiling to make room on top, exposing the bare fluorescent bulbs and wiring. Oh, it was lovely.

We remodeled, repainted, or replaced every single surface in the house—every wall, every ceiling, every floor. We moved the kitchen, tore down walls, built new walls, replaced hundreds of switch plates, and changed light fixtures.

We were too busy fixing things up inside to get to know anyone around us, except for a couple of neighbors who had children the same age as our daughter and the man who stopped to compliment our freshly bulldozed lawn. One neighbor, Rose, told me that when she moved here, her realtor happened to live on her street. He warned her, "It's a nice neighborhood, but we don't neighbor—as a verb." He was right, and that was fine by me. When we shopped for a home, I told our realtor all the amenities I wanted to make my family comfortable, and of course I was concerned about "location, location, location." I wanted a neighborhood that was safe, convenient, and pretty. At that time, I gave very little thought or care to the people who would be my neighbors.

Over the years we've transformed that big, ugly house into a lovely home physically . . . but the real renovation was in my own heart, spiritually. Little did I know that its living room is where I would open my Bible for the first time in decades. Little did I know

> "It's a nice neighborhood, but we don't neighbor— as a verb."

that my first feeble attempts at prayer would be made folding clothes at its laundry room counter. I could not foresee the dark spiritual battles or bright victories and joy these rooms would hold. Little did I know that inside its walls God would teach me first to love Him, then to love my neighbor.

## Martha, Martha

Shortly after Jesus told the parable of the Good Samaritan (Luke 10:30–37) that redefined what it meant to love your neighbor, He traveled the same road between Jericho and Jerusalem where the parable took place—but this time He is the one who needed help. He had no place to spend the night, no fast-food drive-through to feed His entourage.

Jesus stopped at a village called Bethany, about two miles east of Jerusalem, at the home of His very good friend Martha; her sister, Mary; and their brother, Lazarus.

> As Jesus and the disciples continued on their way to Jerusalem, they came to a certain village where a woman named Martha welcomed him into her home. Her sister, Mary, sat at the Lord's

feet, listening to what he taught. But Martha was distracted by the big dinner she was preparing. She came to Jesus and said, "Lord, doesn't it seem unfair to you that my sister just sits here while I do all the work? Tell her to come and help me."

But the Lord said to her, "My dear Martha, you are worried and upset over all these details! There is only one thing worth being concerned about. Mary has discovered it, and it will not be taken away from her."

Luke 10:38–42

Martha, Martha, Martha. What are we going to do with you? I can relate to a woman who bosses Jesus around, because that's usually my first reaction when I don't think He's paying enough attention to my suffering. "Come on, Lord—how much longer am I supposed to take this? I need some heavenly help here!" I complain. I know exactly how Martha feels when I'm working my tail off, waiting for someone to clap for my solo performance.

> We are rarely distracted or over-occupied with loving God or loving our neighbor.

Can we give Martha a break? Martha welcomed Jesus into her home— not just Jesus, but His disciples too— and unquestioningly opened her home to quite a crowd for dinner. If someone didn't make Jesus a meal, He wasn't going to eat. Hers was a necessary service. That's a good thing! A necessary thing! A delightful obedience to the command to love your neighbor!

Yet Martha was distracted by her big dinner plans. The Greek word translated "distracted" is *perispaō*, and it is used only here in the entire Bible. It means to be drawn away and distracted, to be over-occupied or too busy. If Luke was telling the tale of a twenty-first-century woman, he would use this word a lot more . . . a whole lot more! We are distracted by our responsibilities at home and at work, our duties at church, endless activities for our children, our dogged pursuit of fitness and financial stability, and family obligations. We are distracted by texts, tweets, notifications, friend requests, and followers.

We are rarely distracted or over-occupied with loving God or loving our neighbor.

Caught off guard, Martha got off track. She forgot that her most important Guest was her highest priority, and she allowed herself to be distracted by relatively unimportant details. Martha chose crudités over a conversation with Jesus. No one remembers what Martha served for dinner that night, but Sunday school classrooms around the world still teach about Martha, the frazzled hostess.

Martha wasn't unspiritual; she was simply unprepared. Not that she should have been prepared to feed so many mouths without warning, but she should have been prepared to shift gears. Martha's intentions were good, but her timing was off— when Jesus came in, she should have reprioritized, refocused, and rested in the presence of her honored Guest.

Martha gets bonus points because her guest was Jesus: she could love God and love her neighbor at the same time. Wait a minute . . . we can do that too—"I tell you the truth, when you did it to one of the least of these my brothers and sisters, you were doing it to me!" (Matthew 25:40).

Jesus gave Martha a break, so we can too. In Christianese, that special language we speak at church, it's an insult to be labeled a "Martha"—but Jesus loved her: "Jesus loved Martha" (John 11:5).

Martha learned well from Jesus' kind rebuke. When her brother was ill, she didn't boss Jesus around again—she simply sent Him a note saying Lazarus was sick. When Jesus finally came to Bethany, Lazarus had been dead and buried for four days. Martha didn't make the same mistake and stay cooped up in the kitchen making a funeral meal—she ran out to meet Jesus. Her faith was strong even in her sorrow as she said to Jesus, "I have always believed you are the Messiah, the Son of God, the one who has come into the world from God" (John 11:27).

Martha—the so-called unspiritual sister, the cranky one in the kitchen who sassed Jesus and bossed Him around, the frazzled and distracted one—was the first woman to recognize Christ as the Messiah, the Son of God! The first three gospels record Peter's confession that Jesus is the Christ, but John recorded only Martha's. Yay, Martha! Cue the happy music!

> Martha—the so-called unspiritual sister—was the first woman to recognize Christ as the Messiah, the Son of God!

We see Martha back in her familiar role a few days before the crucifixion:

> Six days before the Passover celebration began, Jesus arrived in Bethany, the home of Lazarus—the man he had raised from the dead. A dinner was prepared in Jesus' honor. Martha served, and Lazarus was among those who ate with him. Then Mary took a twelve-ounce jar of expensive perfume made from essence of nard, and she anointed Jesus' feet with it, wiping his feet with her hair. The house was filled with the fragrance.
>
> John 12:1–3

In Jesus' honor, Martha served. Through trial and error and grace, Martha learned to use her gift of serving well. Pastor J. Vernon McGee said,

> What a picture we have here! There is Lazarus alive from the dead and in fellowship with Christ. Then we see Mary sitting at Jesus' feet, growing in grace and in the knowledge of Christ. Then, thirdly, we see Martha serving, putting on a meal. That is her gift and she is exercising it. These are the three essentials in the church today: new life in Christ, worship and adoration, and service. This home at Bethany should be a picture of your church and mine.

All this is in the home where Jesus is with His own. As you know, the church began in the home. It may end in the home . . . where true fellowship with Christ will be found.[1]

Please don't scorn service as a lowly domestic duty. To serve (Greek *diakoneō*) means to wait at a table and offer food and drink to the guests, like Martha did, but it also means to take care of the needs of others, like Jesus did. Jesus used the same word of himself:

> Whoever wants to be a leader among you must be your servant, and whoever wants to be first among you must be the slave of everyone else. For even the Son of Man came not to be served but to serve others and to give his life as a ransom for many.
>
> Mark 10:43–45

Martha can teach us how to find balance between loving service and angrily slaving away.

## Entertaining vs. Hospitality

Some women have a knack for making things beautiful. I am not one of them. My husband is a better decorator than me, and my neighbor Juanita can wave her magic wand over anything and make it sparkle. She owned a store in town where she transformed a hodgepodge of old, new, and repurposed items into beautiful displays. Her eye for color and texture and style amazes me—and it blesses me! She has come into my home and fluffed it to perfection.

Martha had a knack for entertaining. Entertaining looks good, smells good, and feels good. Entertaining

> Entertaining looks good, smells good, and feels good. Entertaining is picture-perfect and Pinterest-worthy.

is picture-perfect and Pinterest-worthy. There are magazines, books, blogs, and television shows dedicated to entertaining. If you've ever been lavishly entertained, you came away feeling impressed. You enjoyed an experience that was a treat to all your senses! Entertainment can be absolutely delightful. If you are an entertainer, you appreciate the thoughtfulness, talent, time, effort, and expense it can require.

Hospitality, on the other hand, can happen in a messy house. It can happen over store-bought cookies with mismatched paper plates—thank you, Lord! The root of the word *hospitality* is the same as the words *hospital* and *hospice*. It is from the Latin for "guest." To practice hospitality is to nurture, strengthen, and serve your guests so that they leave your home physically, spiritually, and emotionally strengthened. If you've ever been treated to lavish hospitality, you can't remember a thing you ate or what the house looked like—but you remember delightful laughter, deep conversations, and disarming authenticity.

> Hospitality can happen in a messy house.

If you entertain without being hospitable, your tension and unrealistic expectations will leave a bad taste in your guests' mouths.

> Don't eat with people who are stingy; don't desire their delicacies. They are always thinking about how much it costs. "Eat and drink," they say, but they don't mean it. You will throw up what little you've eaten, and your compliments will be wasted.
>
> Proverbs 23:6–8

If you are hospitable without a thought to entertaining, your guests might not be overly impressed by your house when they arrive, but you'll make a big impression on their hearts when they leave.

Better a dry crust eaten in peace than a house filled with feasting—and conflict.

Proverbs 17:1

I think God is more concerned with my heart for hosting than my knack for housekeeping. This is the difference between entertaining, which makes me look good, and hospitality, which makes my guests feel good. The goal of inviting a neighbor into your home is extreme hospitality, overwhelming kindness, and extravagant grace . . . not grandeur.

> Entertaining makes me look good; hospitality makes my guests feel good.

When we learn to balance hospitality and entertainment like Martha did, they are powerful tools to love our neighbors.

## That Darned Proverbs 31 Woman

If you've spent any time at all in women's Bible studies, you've surely met that irritatingly intimidating woman in Proverbs 31:10–31. She works happily from morning till night while her husband and children cheer her on. She is generous, encouraging, carefree, and always kind. She's a savvy shopper (she would have been an extreme couponer), industrious, a good seamstress, and a businesswoman who has mastered entertaining and hospitality: "She's skilled in the crafts of home and hearth, diligent in homemaking" (Proverbs 31:19 THE MESSAGE).

Although this passage was written by Lemuel, it was taught to him by his mother: "The sayings of King Lemuel contain this message, which his mother taught him" (Proverbs 31:1).

If Lemuel is a nickname for King Solomon, as most scholars believe, then these messages were taught to him by Bathsheba.

Bathsheba is one of only four women who are included in the genealogy of Jesus (Matthew 1:6). She was also a woman who knew loss and love, conflict and reconciliation, sin and grace—now, *this* is a woman I can relate to!

But do you realize what this means, girlfriends? The Proverbs 31 woman is a mother-in-law's description of the perfect wife for her prince of a son! When she says, "Who can find a virtuous and capable wife?" (v. 10), I think she is bemoaning the fact that this woman does not exist. Solomon had seven hundred wives and three hundred concubines for her to choose from, and she still couldn't find one who met her expectations.

> The Proverbs 31 woman is a mother-in-law's description of the perfect wife for her prince of a son!

As you compare yourself to the Proverbs 31 woman, please remember she does not represent one real day in the life of one real woman. You probably won't spin flax, gather food from afar (unless McDonald's counts), get up before dawn to make breakfast, buy a field, plant a garden, make your own bedspread while wearing a purple robe and a Mona Lisa smile all in one day—unless you have a few servant girls, like she did. The Proverbs 31 woman is the woman we aspire to be, but her list of virtues is not a magnifying mirror we use to examine our flaws. Her daily duties are not a checklist we start anew each morning.

## I Can't Compare

I've just learned to swim—really swim. I could always manage to get myself out of the deep end, but now I can swim laps. One day at the pool there was another woman swimming two lanes over, and I couldn't help but notice that she was fast—incredibly fast, much faster than me. She didn't even come up for breath until she was halfway across the pool, but I came up gasping after three strokes. I tried to focus on kicking with loose ankles and gliding with each choppy stroke, and other important techniques like not dying or alarming the lifeguard, but she whizzed by me again. My concentration and my confidence took a dive. "I'm a beached whale! I must look ridiculous. Who am I kidding, thinking I can swim?" We smiled as she got out of the pool, and I was glad my foggy goggles hid my tears.

Then she took off her flippers.

When we compare ourselves to others, we never have the whole picture. There's more beneath the surface that we can't see, and it skews our perception. We compare our bodies, our accomplishments, our abilities, our spiritual gifts, our families, our jobs, our cars, our vacations, our homes, and our house-keeping. And we don't just compare our homes to the others on our street, we hold them up against glossy magazines, Pinterest boards, and decorating shows. These lofty ideals, which few of us will ever achieve, become convenient excuses for not using our homes to love our neighbors.

Can we be honest about these excuses and just talk about some very practical ways to care for our homes?

## Cleanliness Is Next to Godliness

Okay, that's not in the Bible, but it does make it easier to love your neighbor if your house is cleaned up. This isn't an eat-off-the-floor kind of clean; a simple wipe-off-what-someone-just-ate-off-the-floor will do. Your goal is to be able to invite some-one over without notice, like Lydia did—

> On the Sabbath we went a little way outside the city to a riverbank, where we thought people would be meeting for prayer, and we sat down to speak with some women who had gathered there.

One of them was Lydia from Thyatira, a merchant of expensive purple cloth, who worshiped God. As she listened to us, the Lord opened her heart, and she accepted what Paul was saying. She and her household were baptized, and she asked us to be her guests. "If you agree that I am a true believer in the Lord," she said, "come and stay at my home." And she urged us until we agreed.

Acts 16:13–15

The first thing I notice about Lydia is that she's into purple, like that snazzy Proverbs 31 woman (I am going to buy a purple shirt and see if it makes me act more holy). Lydia is a businesswoman, she loves Jesus, and she's ready to invite people to her house at the drop of a hat. Kinda reminds you of Martha, doesn't she? Lydia's hospitality was a natural continuation of her worship.

> Our goal in caring for our home is that it will be a place of worship, like Lydia's home and Martha's home.

Our goal in caring for our home is that it will be a place of worship, like Lydia's home and Martha's home. Our goal is to maintain our home so that we will not freak out if a neighbor stops by unexpectedly. Our goal is to be able to confidently say to a neighbor, "Would you like to come over for dessert tonight?" Our goal is to focus on the people living around us and provide a venue for us to gather. Our goal is for our guests to be comfortable, not worrying they're going to catch an infectious disease from our sofa. Our goal is to safeguard and safekeep one of the most expensive blessings God loans to us, our home, so that it can be used for His glory. Our goal is to serve our neighbor, in Jesus' honor.

You will use your knees and your elbows to do this. First, spend a lot of time on your knees praying God will give you opportunities to welcome your neighbor into your home. Then, gather some cleaning supplies and apply some elbow grease.

Before you fret about your cluttered bedroom closets, remember that your neighbors don't need a tour of your entire house. You can welcome someone into your home without showing them every nook and cranny. You only have to do one room—that's all! It's likely going to be your living room or kitchen, and you may want to take a look at your front door and have a presentable bathroom.

### Front porch and entryway
- Sweep sidewalk and porch
- Shake out the doormat
- Clean glass door
- Put away any clutter that was abandoned at the front door

### Living room
- Put away anything that doesn't belong (even if you have to temporarily stash it in trash bags or laundry baskets)
- Fold blankets and straighten magazines, discard old newspapers
- Knock down any cobwebs along the ceiling or light fixtures
- Dust furniture
- Clean glass surfaces and pictures
- Vacuum upholstery and flip cushions
- Sweep or vacuum floors; mop hardwood floors

### Kitchen
- Put away unnecessary clutter and dishes
- Wipe cabinets, stovetop, and appliances
- Dust any knickknacks and clean small countertop appliances
- Scour the sink

- Clean floors
- Wipe down the kitchen table and chairs

**Bathroom**

- Put away personal items like toothbrushes, combs, and brushes
- Clean mirror
- Clean sink and countertop
- Clean toilet
- Empty wastebaskets
- Provide ample toilet paper and offer paper towels for drying hands

**General tips**

- Wipe the switch plates, doorknobs, and doorjambs to instantly brighten a room
- Don't use overpowering scents for your guests who are sensitive to strong odors
- Have a plan for overly friendly or unfriendly pets

These tips have been gleaned from homemaking pros as well as the school of hard knocks. I am the one who left the fireplace flue closed and filled my house with smoke minutes before my neighbors and friends arrived. I am the one whose conversation with my neighbor was interrupted by a spider dangling right between us from its web in my kitchen light fixture. I am the one whose holy dog took a slurp from the toilet during our very first prayer at our very first Bible study, then plopped herself in the middle of our group and burped.

## It's Perfect

Whether we live in the projects or a pretty little subdivision, we women want our homes to be nice. We'd like everything to be perfect before we open up the place. Let's face it, friends—it's never gonna happen. Even if we could make our homes look perfect, they are still occupied by imperfect people.

Look at your home with your heart instead of your eyes. Chances are, your neighbors' homes are similar to yours in size, shape, age, condition, and value. They won't be shocked by what they see; in fact, if you focus on their needs instead of your home's needs, they'll be touched. God cares more about what kind of neighbor you are than what kind of house you live in.

So, yeah—you can give up those dreams of a perfect house. You may not have the fanciest furniture or the most modern décor—but your home can be clean and the atmosphere can be welcoming. Whether you love your house or you hate it, it can become an idol that interferes with your worship of the one true God if you hold an improper or unbalanced view of it. Let's lose the excuses that keep us from sharing our homes, and find new meaning in practicing hospitality.

> **Even if we could make our homes look perfect, they are still occupied by imperfect people.**

If we're going to compare ourselves to the Proverbs 31 woman and the Lydias and Marthas of the world, let it be by this sole verse: "Charm is deceptive, and beauty does not last; but a woman who fears the Lord will be greatly praised" (Proverbs 31:30).

Outward beauty doesn't last—in women or the houses they live in. We don't want to be remembered for floral arrangements and fancy cupcakes. Instead, let's be remembered for our love for God, which flows through us to our neighbor—that is the secret of hospitality and the beauty of entertaining.

# Next Best Steps

1. What is your favorite home you've lived in? What's your favorite neighborhood you've lived in? As you've chosen where to live, did you consider the neighbors or just the neighborhood?

2. What distracts you from paying attention to people? How can you refocus and realign your priorities?

3. Do you relate to Martha's frustration when she was doing all the work? Where do you feel like you're working all alone, with no one to help? Could this be an unimportant area that needs to be done differently?

4. Do you see service as an honor or a duty? Do you serve happily or do you feel put upon? Where do you most enjoy serving?

5. Are you an entertainer, or do you practice hospitality—or have you figured out how to balance both? Think of a time when you or your host was stressed by entertaining. Remember a time when you were refreshed by someone's hospitality.

6. On a scale of 1–10, how prepared are you to welcome guests into your home—in Jesus' honor?

| 1 | 3 | 5 | 7 | 10 |
|---|---|---|---|---|
| There should be a TV show about my house | Mortified | Slightly embarrassed | Just a sec while I shove this mess under the couch | Come on in! |

7. How much time do you spend caring for your home each week? Do you feel this is excessive, not enough, or just right? Does your family agree?

# Your Neighborhood
# Strategy

It was a typical Sunday afternoon on a beautiful spring day. After a nice service at church, my family ate lunch together, then went their separate ways—my husband worked in the yard, I paid bills (and maybe checked Facebook just a little), our daughter was in her room.

From my desk, I thought I heard shouting coming from the back of our house—it was very faint, but it sounded like, "Help! Help!" I ran to the back door and saw our neighbor standing on his side of the fence shouting, "Help!"—but he was pointing to *my* yard. I followed his pointing and more shouting, and then I saw David. It was my husband who needed help, and he shouted, "I'm on fire!" His pants had caught on fire as he was burning leaves in our backyard.

I have no idea how they got there, but neighbors immediately appeared on our back deck. Tori ran inside to the bathroom, pulled towels off the rack, wet them in the sink, and ran outside to put them on David's legs. To this day she doesn't know why she went out to her garage, where she then heard shouts for help. Her husband, Jim—a doctor—spoke so calmly and gave directions. They helped get David to the car and told us what to do when we got to the emergency room.

At the hospital, one of the emergency room nurses was a neighbor I had met when I knocked on her door and invited her over for coffee. Monica gave us her cell phone number and told us to call any time. One neighbor brought us a plate of still-warm-from-the-oven brownies when she learned what happened, and another kindly delayed jackhammering their patio so David could recuperate peacefully.

I used to think I didn't have time to love my neighbors, but now I know I don't have time *not* to love my neighbors! Thankfully, my husband's serious burns healed completely and left only a scar as a reminder. It was a very difficult time, but it wasn't the end of the world.

The end of the world as we know it can happen when a routine household chore lands you in the emergency room or when an officer knocks on the door in the middle of the night. Our world can be turned upside down when the doctor calls but she won't give your test results over the phone. Life as we know it will never be the same when divorce splinters a family, drug addiction robs a mother of her child, a job cannot be found so a home is lost. Dreams are dashed every day in your neighborhood when a once-rosy future becomes suddenly bleak.

## The End of the World As We Know It

When we come to the end of ourselves, we experience our own personal apocalypse. But there's a bigger bang coming soon.

Christ's return will turn everything we've ever known upside down. The second coming could be here any second!

People have been predicting the end of the world since the beginning of the world. Remember all the hype about the Mayan calendar that foretold the end of the world on December 21, 2012? In my own little city, a billboard proclaimed the end of the world would be May 21, 2011. Prepping for a zombie apocalypse, nuclear disaster, or alien invasion keeps a lot of people busy these days.

> I don't have time **not** to love my neighbors!

The apostles believed the end of the world was coming soon. They didn't try to second-guess the second coming or waste time figuring out the end-times timeline—yet they lived each day as if their beloved Jesus might walk in the door at any minute. They were less concerned with the question of *when* the world might end and more concerned with the question of *what* they would do each day until that happened. They saw each precious day that God withholds His judgment as another chance for their neighbors to be saved.

The end *is* near, nearer now than when you poured your morning coffee. So what? What should we do? Should we buy bottled water and build bomb shelters? Or should we take a good look at how we live and what kind of people we are?

> Since everything will be destroyed in this way, what kind of people ought you to be? You ought to live holy and godly lives. . . . So then, dear friends, since you are looking forward to this, make every effort to be found spotless, blameless and at peace with him.
>
> 2 Peter 3:11, 14 NIV

What kind of people ought we to be? How should we then live? That is the only question we should be asking in light of

> What kind
> of people ought
> we to be? How
> should we then
> live? That is the
> only question we
> should be asking
> in light of the end
> of the world.

the end of the world. This isn't the time to quiver in fear. This is the time to ask, "Am I at peace with God?"

Peter didn't leave us in suspense, twiddling our thumbs until the world comes crashing down. Until that day comes, he outlined four specific steps that will become your neighborhood strategy. By studying Peter's life, we'll see how he developed his plan the hard way. Following these four steps will help you to live a holy and godly life so that you will be found spotless, blameless, and at peace with God when Jesus comes again—you, and hopefully quite a few of your neighbors too.

## Strategy #1: Pray Earnestly

The end of the world is coming soon. Therefore, be earnest and disciplined in your prayers.

1 Peter 4:7

"Soon." This time frame is ambiguous, unclear, and intentionally vague. Jesus told a parable about a man who would return "soon" from a long trip, leaving his workers instructions about the work they were to do in his absence. Peter heard Jesus tell this story:

You, too, must keep watch! For you don't know when the master of the household will return—in the evening, at midnight, before dawn, or at daybreak. Don't let him find you sleeping when he arrives without warning.

Mark 13:35–36

A few days later, Peter celebrated the Passover meal with Jesus, then went with Him to an olive grove called Gethsemane. Jesus told him, "Sit here while I go and pray. . . . Stay here and keep watch with me" (Mark 14:32, 34).

In that hour in the Garden of Gethsemane, Jesus needed Peter as He had never needed another human being before in His life. Jesus knew He would soon be spiritually crushed, emotionally battered, financially robbed, physically beaten, and relationally betrayed. How did Peter respond to his friend's plea for prayer?

> Then he returned and found the disciples asleep. He said to Peter, "Simon, are you asleep? Couldn't you watch with me even one hour? Keep watch and pray, so that you will not give in to temptation. For the spirit is willing, but the body is weak."
>
> Then Jesus left them again and prayed the same prayer as before. When he returned to them again, he found them sleeping, for they couldn't keep their eyes open. And they didn't know what to say.
>
> When he returned to them the third time, he said, "Go ahead and sleep. Have your rest. But no—the time has come. The Son of Man is betrayed into the hands of sinners."
>
> Mark 14:37–41

Three times Peter fell asleep on the job. And not just any job—Peter fell asleep during one of the most important assignments he'd ever been given! Yet this man eventually wrote 1 Peter 4:7, urging us to be "earnest and disciplined in our prayers." This is why I love Peter! Peter gives me hope for my hapless self. If he can catch on, I might be able to catch on too.

In various translations, the words Peter used to describe how we are to pray in 1 Peter 4:7 are interpreted as earnest, disciplined, alert, sober-minded, wide-awake (love that one!), serious, and watchful. Would you like to see an example of this kind of prayer at work? Look no further than Jesus, who beautifully showed us the power of "earnest and disciplined" prayer in the same passage where Peter slept. This was Jesus' state of mind at that moment: "He became deeply troubled and distressed" (Mark 14:33).

The Greek word translated "troubled" is *ekthambeō,* and it means to be struck with terror, alarmed thoroughly, struck with amazement, or astounded. "Distressed" is the word *adēmoneō,* and it means in great distress or anguish, depressed.

Think of your worst day . . . times ten. Have you felt terror? Trouble? Distress? Depression? Oh, honey— Jesus understands. He's right there with you in your living room, remembering His own dark moments in an olive grove. If this gives you comfort, imagine how lost and alone your neighbor who does not know Christ must feel during her worst day.

> Jesus understands. He's right there with you in your living room, remembering His own dark moments in an olive grove.

There's no perfect prayer formula; there are no perfect prayers or prayers. When you're losing your mind, prayer helps you keep your head. And when you come to your very own end times—the end of a dream, the end of hope, the end of yourself—earnest and disciplined conversation with God will bring His presence, His peace, and His power into your situation.

Your first neighborhood strategy is to practice earnest and disciplined prayers for your neighbors. They too are suffering spiritually, emotionally, financially, physically, and relationally. Do not be found sleeping on the job.

## Strategy #2: Love Deeply

Peter lived in daily expectation of Christ's return, and so should we. We should all be preppers, survivalists who make preparations to survive a widespread catastrophe. But instead of stockpiling supplies, Peter said we should show love for each other:

> Most important of all, continue to show deep love for each other.
>
> 1 Peter 4:8

This isn't your average, ordinary love: This is deep love, earnest love, fervent love. Peter used the Greek word *ektenēs* to describe this love. It means to stretch out your hand or "stretched out." Deep love is unconditional, unceasing, unwavering, and unrelenting. It is undeserved love, uncomfortable love—the kind of love that stretches your heart to the breaking point. This kind of love is a side effect of salvation, Peter explained,

> You were cleansed from your sins when you obeyed the truth, so now you must show sincere love to each other as brothers and sisters. Love each other deeply with all your heart.
>
> 1 Peter 1:22

We use the word *love* pretty loosely, don't we? I love my husband. I love my daughter. I love my dog. I love peanut butter. I love my root-lifter spray mousse. There are four different Greek words we translate into English as "love":

- *Éros*: intimate love, attraction, or sexual desire. Eros was the Greek god of love and is the root of the word *erotic*.
- *Storgê*: natural affection such as that felt by parents for offspring. Used almost exclusively for family relationships.
- *Phileō*: friendship or affectionate love, including loyalty to friends, family, and community. Root of *Philadelphia*, City of Brotherly Love.
- *Agápe*: unconditional love, to love dearly. The feeling of being content or holding in high regard.

The words *éros* and *storgê* are not used in the Bible, but *agápe* and *phileō* are used hundreds of times. John 3:16 is about *agápe* love: "For this is how God loved the world: He gave his one and only Son, so that everyone who believes in him will not perish but have eternal life."

God loved us so much that He stretched out His hand and gave us His Son. Jesus loved us so much that He stretched out His arms to be nailed to the cross. Peter is calling us to the kind of love that stretches out and gives something precious and costly of itself.

Peter wasn't always the world's greatest lover of people. He fought with the other disciples about who was the greatest (Luke 9:46–48). He wouldn't enter the home or associate with anyone who wasn't also a Jew (Acts 10). Peter was also a mathematician who carefully counted offenses given and pardons received. One day he asked Jesus how many times he should forgive someone who sinned against him, magnanimously suggesting that seven was the max on the forgiveness meter. (Before you judge Peter, please know the Jewish rabbis of the day taught that three times was sufficient.) Like a math teacher patiently instructing a student, Jesus replied that unlimited forgiveness—"seventy times seven times"—was the solution. Peter eventually understood and offered this equation: "Love covers a multitude of sins" (1 Peter 4:8).

Love doesn't point out every error (that's not what Cupid's arrows are for!). Agápe love doesn't rehash every wrong deed, but it isn't naïve either. Agápe love looks sin square in the eye and says, "That was wrong, and it hurt. But I forgive you, I love you, and I pray that God would bless your life." Agápe love causes us to release our pain to our heavenly Father and allow Him to heal us so that we can love freely and deeply again. If Peter—a quarrelsome, prejudiced, and resentful man—can be transformed by the power of God into a peaceful, accepting, and forgiving person, then there is hope for me!

So what would our neighborhoods look like if we deeply loved our neighbor? Our second neighborhood strategy is to allow God to stretch our hearts with a love so deep it can't be contained.

## Strategy #3: Share Cheerfully

Even after I quit smoking and could welcome people freely into my home, other bad habits like selfishness, laziness, slothfulness, and fear barred my door. One day a business associate who lived across the country casually mentioned, "I'll see you next week." What did that mean, I asked? I wasn't planning on seeing him next week. Next week was the week before school started, the week when I fulfilled our daughter's what-I-did-on-my-summer-vacation memories, a week of hectic back-to-school shopping and harried you're-on-my-last-nerve clashes. "My wife and I are coming next week. We're staying at your house for six days," he replied. "Didn't your husband tell you?"

Um, no, he hadn't. My husband failed to mention he had invited this man and his wife, whom I had never met, to our home to stay for six already stressful days. And did I mention that his rock-star wife (literally—she sang in a band) was young enough to be my daughter? I was more than slightly annoyed.

We spent the first ten minutes upon their arrival discussing her tattoos. We spent the next ten minutes admiring her seriously punked-out hair while I tried to tousle my frumpy grays.

We spent the rest of the time having a blast.

Hannah is one of the sweetest women I've ever met, and we've remained close friends as well as co-workers many years later. And, as a permanent humbling reminder of the blessing God can pour out on a reluctantly hospitable, barely sociable believer, they sent me a #1 Hostess trophy as a thank-you gift! Oh, if they only knew.

Peter's secret ingredient to the third neighborhood strategy is "cheerfulness," a quality I sorely lacked. It means "without murmuring or grudging," with a cheerful and willing mind:

> Cheerfully share your home with those who need a meal or a place to stay.
>
> 1 Peter 4:9

Perhaps Peter learned this tip when he helped Jesus serve dinner to a few thousand guests. In typical Peter fashion, we'll see him mess things up himself before he can preach it to us!

**Most of us react badly to a bad day. But not Jesus.**

The story of Jesus feeding five thousand men (not even counting women and children) is found in all four gospels (Matthew 14; Mark 6; Luke 9; John 6). Jesus' popularity was growing. Throngs of people began to follow Him everywhere He went. Jesus was grieving the murder of His dear friend and relative, John the Baptist, yet people pressed in on Him from every side, wanting to touch Him, demanding his attention, and asking Him to fix their problems. As Jesus tried to get away with His disciples to find a quiet place to rest, the crowds clamored for His attention. There was no time to eat, let alone pray or mourn.

You could say Jesus was having a bad day.

And that's okay. We all have bad days. Most of us, however, react badly to a bad day. But not Jesus. He stopped. He looked into His neighbors' eyes, and was moved with compassion. He saw people who were lost, directionless, searching. He sat with them all day and poured himself into them. He was still serving cheerfully when the disciples interrupted—

> Late in the afternoon his disciples came to him and said, "This is a remote place, and it's already getting late. Send the crowds

away so they can go to the nearby farms and villages and buy something to eat."

But Jesus said, "You feed them."

"With what?" they asked. "We'd have to work for months to earn enough money to buy food for all these people!"

Mark 6:35–37

I love the disciples' brand of compassion: Let's send everyone away so they can fend for themselves! Can you blame them? They were physically tired. They were emotionally exhausted. They were financially strapped. They were unprepared. They were inconvenienced. And you know what? All of their excuses were valid. Your own excuses for not cheerfully sharing your home may, in fact, be true.

But Jesus will take whatever you offer Him, and He will multiply your scraps into something you can cheerfully serve your neighbor. Somehow they managed to round up five loaves of bread and two fish. Jesus took their little offering, looked to heaven, and blessed it. He divided the bread into smaller pieces, but the meal was multiplied instead. He kept giving and giving the bread to the disciples, who ran from blanket to blanket feeding family after family until everyone had eaten all they wanted with leftovers to spare.

If the Holy Spirit can transform Peter from a hostile grumbler to a gracious host, if He can help me change from a closet smoker to someone who regularly invites neighbors into my home, then He can certainly help you have one friend over for coffee or a bowl of ice cream. There is hope for us all!

## Strategy #4: Serve Faithfully

I used to think my spiritual gifts were just for me, for my personal pleasure and enjoyment. I love to speak to women and teach the Bible—some of my most rewarding, fulfilling, and exciting moments are spent with my Bible and notebook coming up with new ways to explain timeless principles. I am continually amazed at the joy I receive every time I serve others with one of the spiritual gifts God has given me. With grace upon grace, God rewards us with success, pleasure, and fruitfulness when we accept His gifts and offer them back to serve His people. We've talked at length about identifying your spiritual gifts and how to use them in your neighborhood.

> God has given each of you a gift from his great variety of spiritual gifts. Use them well to serve one another.
>
> 1 Peter 4:10

God gave spiritual gifts to Peter like apostleship, tongues, speaking, evangelism, healing, teaching, and knowledge. Peter was uniquely gifted at speaking. Trouble was, he didn't always know what to say! Peter didn't let that stop him from opening his mouth and inserting his foot on a regular basis—

> From then on Jesus began to tell his disciples plainly that it was necessary for him to go to Jerusalem, and that he would suffer many terrible things at the hands of the elders, the leading priests, and the teachers of religious law. He would be killed, but on the third day he would be raised from the dead.
>
> But Peter took him aside and began to reprimand him for saying such things. "Heaven forbid, Lord," he said. "This will never happen to you!"
>
> Jesus turned to Peter and said, "Get away from me, Satan! You are a dangerous trap to me. You are seeing things merely from a human point of view, not from God's."
>
> Matthew 16:21–23

I can just see Peter rolling his eyes at Jesus, taking His elbow and leading the poor, misled Messiah aside so the other disciples couldn't hear their conversation. "Suffering? Crucifixion? Heaven forbid!" Jesus' harsh reply shows the serious consequences of speaking without understanding. A few days later, Peter still hadn't learned to hold his tongue:

> Six days later Jesus took Peter, James, and John, and led them up a high mountain to be alone. As the men watched, Jesus' appearance was transformed, and his clothes became dazzling white, far whiter than any earthly bleach could ever make them. Then Elijah and Moses appeared and began talking with Jesus.
>
> Peter exclaimed, "Rabbi, it's wonderful for us to be here! Let's make three shelters as memorials—one for you, one for Moses, and one for Elijah." He said this because he didn't really know what else to say, for they were all terrified.
>
> Then a cloud overshadowed them, and a voice from the cloud said, "This is my dearly loved Son. Listen to him."
>
> Mark 9:2–7

As usual, Peter provides us with a good example of a bad example. This is why I love this guy: He's so much like me! If only I could take back every hasty word, every hurtful statement, every unnecessary mumble that has escaped my lips.

> **When your neighbors pour out their woes, don't rush to say everything will be okay. Sometimes it isn't okay, and they know it.**

When you don't know what else to say, consider listening instead! When your neighbors pour out their woes, don't rush to say everything will be okay. Sometimes it isn't okay, and they know it. When you're talking to a neighbor, talk to God the entire time and listen for His mind, His heart, His eyes.

When Peter used his own words, Jesus rebuked him and called him "Satan." When Peter spoke without thinking, God himself reprimanded him. Take it from a man who heard the voice of God in person, your spiritual gifts must be submitted to the Lord and used for His glory, or they will be of no use to you or anyone else.

But when Peter submitted his gifts to the Lord and was filled with the Holy Spirit, God transformed Peter from a loud-mouthed loose cannon into an apostle who could write these words to us today—

> Do you have the gift of speaking? Then speak as though God himself were speaking through you. Do you have the gift of helping others? Do it with all the strength and energy that God supplies. Then everything you do will bring glory to God through Jesus Christ. All glory and power to him forever and ever! Amen.
>
> 1 Peter 4:11

Your fourth and final neighborhood strategy is to use your spiritual gifts to serve your neighbors faithfully. Submit your gifts to the power and leading of the Holy Spirit, and allow Him to use you to bring glory to God through Jesus Christ.

## The End Is Here

Today, the end is near. Tomorrow, the end may be here. Christ may return with a trumpet shout, or we could be called home to meet our Maker. It is not a question of *if* but of *when*. And the only question we ought to be asking until that day comes is, "How should I then live?"

What kind of neighbor should I be? What should my relationships with my neighbors look like? What kinds of conversations should I be having with my neighbors? How many times do I have to forgive my neighbor's barking dog or loud parties? How hard do I have to work in my neighborhood?

Peter will tell us, and he earned the right to write these words without wincing:

> Be careful to live properly among your unbelieving neighbors. Then even if they accuse you of doing wrong, they will see your honorable behavior, and they will give honor to God when he judges the world.
>
> 1 Peter 2:12

Pray earnestly. Love deeply. Share cheerfully. Serve faithfully.
In the end, it's not about us.
It's not even really about our neighbors.
When the end is finally here, it will be all about Jesus.

# Next Best Steps

1. Have you ever experienced an "end of the world as you know it" moment? What happened? How did you get through it? Are any of your neighbors going through something similar?

2. Read warnings that the end of the world is coming soon in Mark 13; 1 Thessalonians 5:1–3; and Revelation 21:1–4. How has the two-thousand-plus-year wait lessened our sense of urgency?

3. Read Luke 12:16–21. Do you think people are prone to "eat, drink, and be merry" because they think they have plenty of years to enjoy life?

4. Use your neighborhood map to pray specifically, earnestly, and diligently over the homes closest to you. Choose one home a day to remember in prayer.

5. How can you stretch your love toward a neighbor whose world is collapsing? What will it cost you?

6. Have your gifts ever gotten you into trouble? What do you need to do to surrender your gifts for God's glory? What gifts, abilities, and resources has God given you that you can cheerfully share with others?

7. If you knew Jesus was coming next week—or you were going to see Him!—what would you do differently in your neighborhood?

# A Word of Warning and
# a Message of Hope

In just a few hours, a dozen neighbors and friends were going to ring my doorbell expecting me to teach them something out of the Bible. The house was clean enough and someone else was bringing a snack, so that was covered. But what in the world were we going to talk about? Ignoring gazillions of exceptional Bible study resources, I had decided to prepare my own lesson on the Holy Spirit. Yikes—the *whole* Holy Spirit, in a forty-five-minute lesson!

And to make matters worse, through a combination of plain ol' procrastination and other pressing deadlines, I had one day to accomplish what usually took me a couple of weeks. "Dear Lord," I prayed, "I really (I mean *really*) need your help. Can you show me something about yourself that I can share with my friends?"

I brewed a pot of coffee, fired up my computer, and pulled out my favorite reference books. For the first couple of hours, I had a sense of hopeful expectation—I was sure God was going to show up big time, blow my mind with a huge revelation, and wrap up my lesson in time for lunch. Instead, my brain was frozen and my fingers were still. I couldn't string two thoughts together. I had no idea how to explain the enormity and complexity of the Holy Spirit.

When lunchtime came and went, panic began to rise. Several urgent things came up that needed my undivided attention, like organizing my canned goods, sorting laundry, and checking Facebook. As darkness fell, I couldn't see straight but I still had nothing. Zip. Zero. Zilch.

"This is an attack of the enemy," I declared. "I will not be defeated!" I vowed to fight my way through it. I opened my Bible with renewed vigor, determined to make this lesson work. The battle was torturous, laborious, and didn't feel very victorious.

At some point during the long and unproductive night, I had another thought: *Maybe this is my fault.*

I'm a deadline-driven procrastinator who had let this go until the last minute. The last couple of weeks I had been distracted not only from studying but also from my own quiet time with the Lord. I deserved this. Maybe He was putting me in the corner for a little time-out, so next time I would take more time to prepare. I was dealing with the aftermath of my own mistakes. I promised I would try harder . . . but I wasn't really sure I could.

Nevertheless, I felt a responsibility to my guests to prepare something—anything!—for them. I worked into the night, and by 2:00 a.m. I had a few pages of notes and a handout ready for my girls. But when I blearily awoke early the next morning and went to print the materials, my computer would not cooperate. I rebooted it and prayed over it and even cursed it, but nothing helped. There was no way that paper was going to come out of that printer that day.

It was then that I heard a soft whisper, "What if this is an opportunity in disguise?"

My computer was vexed . . . or was it blessed? What if God had something else in mind for our time together that day? Wouldn't it be just like God to send the Holy Spirit for a personal visit instead of sending me a lesson plan about Him?

I regrouped and re-prayed. "Lord, this obviously isn't going according to my plan. Do you have another plan? Help me to be sensitive to this Holy Spirit.I've been studying, and show me how to follow in your footsteps." I felt frustrated and inadequate, and my fears were only slightly appeased by curiosity at what the Lord might be up to. I dedicated the day to Him and asked Him to work in spite of me if He couldn't work through me.

The doorbell rang and in they came—these women who were once strangers, now comfortably ensconced in my living room and in my life. Since I didn't have a lesson, I let the Lord and the ladies take the lead. Everyone was in a talkative mood so I let them talk, not interrupting to get on with the study like I usually did. They didn't seem to miss my detailed teaching notes and full-color handouts. Jennifer talked about the last lesson and how it had impacted her. Linda told a hilarious story, and Mary Ann made us all cry. They encouraged one another.

And you know what? It was one of the best Bible studies we ever had. I had been praying for deeper friendships among us, and that morning I watched as this prayer was answered.

I learned that God can make my words flow, and He can dam them up. He can jam printers just to give me pause. He can redeem my mistakes and use them for His purposes. He can even help me overcome the enemy.

You know what else I learned?

Sometimes the only difference between an attack, an aftermath, or an opportunity is how we *answer*.

## The Attack of Spiritual Persecution

Spiritual persecution is real, this I know. As surely as I believe in good, I believe in evil.

> For we are not fighting against flesh-and-blood enemies, but against evil rulers and authorities of the unseen world, against mighty powers in this dark world, and against evil spirits in the heavenly places.
>
> Ephesians 6:12

I should warn you that the devil hates this whole "love" thing God is always talking about. Every time you knock on a neighbor's door in a gesture of Christian love, you stir a hornet's nest of "evil rulers and authorities of the unseen world" who will do everything they can to stop you. Jesus may have come so that we may have a rich and satisfying life—but there is a thief who comes to steal and kill and destroy. Don't for one minute think the devil will sit idly by while you go love your neighbor!

What does his attack look like? It might look like a fight with your husband that anyone walking down the street could easily overhear. It might look like a police car in front of your house when your child is out of control. It might look like discouragement, or an incident that makes you feel disqualified to love your neighbor. Self-doubt and criticism may weigh you down so that you don't see how you could possibly do anyone any good.

> The devil hates this whole "love" thing God is always talking about.

It might look like an abnormal mammogram or mysterious skin rash that torments you day and night. The devil specifically asked if he could pester Job with physical ailments, and he still uses this attack regularly. It's not because you've done something bad, but because you're up to something good!

It might look like an argument with your neighbors over an aggressive dog or unmown grass or a car parked in your space—and these annoyances can get under your skin and make you want to give them a piece of your mind. You might be the one calling the police on them, or reporting them to City Hall for code violations.

We must fight this external battle with truth—knowing that this is opposition to God himself, not us. We may be caught in the middle, but we know Who comes out on top! The devil has strategies and an attack plan, but wrapped around that verse is our best Defense:

> We may be caught in the middle, but we know Who comes out on top!

> Put on all of God's armor so that you will be able to stand firm against all strategies of the devil. . . . Therefore, put on every piece of God's armor so you will be able to resist the enemy in the time of evil. Then after the battle you will still be standing firm.
>
> Ephesians 6:11, 13

When we step off our front porches into our neighborhoods in the name of Christ, we had better beware. This is too important for the devil not to care!

## The Aftermath of My Participation

Sometimes I give the devil a break and do his job for him. I get so wrapped up in myself that I don't see the needs of others. I neglect my responsibilities, I give in to my selfishness, and I decide to do things my way. God takes me to task when I misbehave.

> "My child, don't make light of the Lord's discipline, and don't give up when he corrects you. For the Lord disciplines those he loves, and he punishes each one he accepts as his child." As you

189

endure this divine discipline, remember that God is treating you as his own children. Who ever heard of a child who is never disciplined by its father?

Hebrews 12:5–7

I need a different kind of weapon when I'm fighting against my own self, and thankfully God offers protection for that, too.

Remove your dark deeds like dirty clothes, and put on the shining armor of right living. Because we belong to the day, we must live decent lives for all to see. Don't participate in the darkness. . . . Instead, clothe yourself with the presence of the Lord Jesus Christ. And don't let yourself think about ways to indulge your evil desires.

Romans 13:12–14

If spiritual persecution is an external battle, my personal participation is an internal battle. Good fences make good neighbors, isn't that what they say? It's hard to admit, but I don't always feel like loving my neighbors. Sometimes I want to be alone. Sometimes I don't want to spend the time. Sometimes I don't want the hassle. I have plenty of my own objections and fears about getting involved in people's lives.

We must fight this internal battle with honor. Be thoughtful. Keep your grass mowed. Shut your dog up—please! Carry little doggie litter bags. Take cookies to new people (put the doggie bag down first). Drive the speed limit. Look out for people. Be aware, and begin to care.

Never pay back evil with more evil. Do things in such a way that everyone can see you are honorable. Do all that you can to live in peace with everyone.

Romans 12:17–18

Use your heads as you live and work among outsiders. Don't miss a trick. Make the most of every opportunity. Be gracious in your speech. The goal is to bring out the best in others in a conversation, not put them down, not cut them out.

Colossians 4:5–6 The Message

I should also warn you that you're on the hook now that you've read this book. You have no excuse for not loving your neighbor, and you don't even have to be weird while doing it. Please don't let this become a nice book about theology that just sits on your shelf. Put it into action on your street. Don't make me pull out James 4:17! We must fight this internal battle with diligence.

## The Opportunity of Purification

And then there are times when God needs to purify me of something that's holding me back from His greatness. Sometimes a little sin I've let slip in keeps me from enjoying the freedom and fullness of life He desires—then He lovingly turns up the heat in order to burn off my impurities and insecurities. Or there may be a new aspect of His personality that I will only grasp through a trial. Hard times can be opportunities to let go of my agenda and lean into His plans. Spiritual persecution is an external battle and personal participation is an internal battle, but God's purification is an eternal battle.

> I will bring that group through the fire and make them pure. I will refine them like silver and purify them like gold. They will call on my name, and I will answer them. I will say, "These are my people," and they will say, "The Lord is our God."
>
> Zechariah 13:9

We experience the external attack of spiritual *persecution*. We experience the internal aftermath of our own *participation*. And we experience the eternal opportunity for *purification*.

191

It's hard to tell these apart; the circumstances can look identical. The emotions may be the same. In the middle of persecution, participation, and purification, we will feel afraid and miserable.

I must warn you that if you've decided to love your neighbor without being weird, you will experience a spiritual attack. You will experience the aftermath of your own actions in your neighborhood. And God will give you the opportunity to grow closer to Him in the process—you will never rely upon Him more than when you approach your neighbor's door.

> I must warn you that if you've decided to love your neighbor without being weird, you will experience a spiritual attack.

The outcome depends on how you respond.

Will you give up? Will you shrink in fear? Will you hide in shame? Or will you emerge from your front door stronger and braver, ready to face your little corner of the world?

## A Message of Hope

Trying to expand beyond my church circles, I joined a volunteer organization that raises money for our local hospital. I met incredibly bright and dedicated women who serve countless hours to provide free mammograms, colonoscopies, medications, and more through a cancer care fund. This secular civic club loved their Robert's Rules of Order, ending meetings on time, and making a difference in the world.

Our annual fundraiser was held on a Sunday morning, and the participants asked if we could pray before it began. Someone motioned that we open with prayer, someone else seconded the motion, everyone in favor said, "Aye!" but Karen said, "Nay!"

I didn't know Karen very well, only that she worked very hard and was willing to say hard things. If anyone was ever going to go against the popular vote, it was going to be Karen. She was plainspoken but outspoken, and she had a problem with the prayer. Karen worried that non-Christians would be offended by a prayer and wondered if we could say a more general "blessing" instead. She was quickly overruled.

"Now, who's going to pray?" the president asked. I was already doing a lot of praying . . . praying God would somehow work this out without getting me involved. The women looked back and forth at each other, raising their eyebrows and shrugging their shoulders.

"I could pray," I said quietly, hoping no one heard.

But they had heard me. "Yes, Amy can pray! She goes to church all the time!" The fact that most of them did too was irrelevant—but this only increased Karen's concerns for the people who didn't go to church.

"Can you just leave God and Christ out of it?" she asked.

"Ummm . . . no, I cannot." I gulped.

The room erupted as they rose to my defense. The president declared, "She's a Christian, she'll say a Christian prayer." Someone motioned that I say the prayer, someone else seconded the motion, everyone in favor said, "Aye!" and this time no one said, "Nay!"

My prayer didn't offend anyone, and at the fundraiser Karen and I had our first real, personal conversation. I learned she was born in Europe, attended a private women's liberal-arts college in the northeastern United States, then graduated with a degree in general liberal arts and humanities from a university in Brussels, whose mission is to provide a "humanistic approach to intellectual inquiry . . . in an open and tolerant environment." Her home country was predominantly Catholic but her family rarely attended mass. In her home country, a religious wedding didn't even count unless the couple had previously been legally married in a civil ceremony. Ahhh, this was beginning to make sense. She was motivated by kindness, not callousness.

She met her husband while living in New York, but they were living in D.C. on 9/11. With two beloved cities under attack, they moved to the relative safety of his hometown. Yeah—my hometown. You remember? The whitest, least diverse, least open and tolerant environment you can find. No wonder her opinions and input were out-of-this-world: She had actually experienced the *real* world!

> The second-most important command comes full circle, from our neighbor's cry to God's ear to our doorstep.

Karen and her husband visited a few local churches and hadn't found one that felt quite right, but she had a soft and seeking heart. "If you're interested, I have a neighborhood Bible study in my home," I told her. "There are women from lots of different churches, and some who don't go to church at all. Would you like to join us?"

So she did. She's been a regular guest in my home for several years, and I in hers—I count her among my close friends. She doesn't come to every Bible study, but most. In her typical fashion that I love and appreciate, Karen doesn't hesitate to tell me when we don't see eye to eye—as in this email she sent after I announced our next topic:

*Dear Amy,*

*God is good: He listens and delivers! Last night at dinner, I told my husband how I've missed your neighborhood Bible study, and that I had a ho-hum year because I didn't make enough time for it. While I did have several conflicts, I wasn't very keen on last year's topics and books, and really wished for a straight-from-the-Bible study.*

*Arthur responded that, if it means that much, I should go. With that, here is your email announcing new dates*

*and a straightforward Bible study—from my heart to God's
and to yours!*
*Can't wait to see you in February! Thank you!*

*Love,*
*Karen*

Karen's story went from "Can you just leave God and Christ out of it?" to getting into God's Word together. In my living room! A friendship that began with a debate over prayer now includes answered prayer. The second-most important command comes full circle, from our neighbor's cry to God's ear to our doorstep.

Will you answer her call by obeying His command?

## Before and After

If your heart is pounding as you read these words, you'll understand the excitement of these women who contacted me about starting front-porch ministry in their very own neighborhoods—

- "God has been talking to me for several months now about starting some kind of gathering in my home, in my neighborhood. . . ."
- "I feel the Lord leading me to start a neighborhood Bible study. . . ."
- "God has laid it on my heart to start a community women's ministry. . . ."
- "It's exciting for me to pursue this venue and know that God will use it to further His kingdom. . . ."
- "I am going to meet my neighbors. I feel that is how God is calling me to light my world. . . ."

Is God stirring your heart, directing you, nudging you, convicting you about following His footsteps off your front porch?

There is a risk. Women will actually see some of your dirty laundry, dirty floors, or dirty dishes. You will make mistakes.

If you dwell there, if you let your fears become excuses like I did, if you delay and disobey, if you wait until your calendar is clear and you have memorized the Old Testament prophets, soon you will sound like these very same women just a few weeks later—

- "I don't have much experience with what to do with non-believers. . . ."
- "I work full time and my schedule varies from week to week. . . ."
- "I have been struggling with what to do and how to do it, and Satan has been working overtime to discourage me. . . ."
- "I don't want to commit the time. However, I think about it all the time. . . ."
- "I am not sure if this will be successful. . . ."
- "I'm scared as my outreach has usually been a bit more one-on-one with my hairdresser, the lady I see every week at the grocery store, that type of thing. . . ."

Oh, how I relate to these dear sisters! They couldn't concoct an excuse I haven't already used. An English major could diagram their statements and tell us what went wrong: The subject changed from *God* to *I*. Girlfriends, we cannot reach out to our neighbors unless we are clinging to God.

> Girlfriends, we cannot reach out to our neighbors unless we are clinging to God.

## Now, Go

Don't bother asking God *if* He wants you to love your neighbor: He does! God is not going to give you a grace pass on loving your neighbor. It's His second most important priority and His plan to reach the world with the Gospel, one neighbor at a time.

Just ask Him *how*. You can do it without being weird, but it still might be hard.

> But you should keep a clear mind in every situation. Don't be afraid of suffering for the Lord. Work at telling others the Good News, and fully carry out the ministry God has given you.
>
> 2 Timothy 4:5

Many women have told me they've prayed for their neighbors for years, and they're excited to learn ways to interact with women they've only interceded for from afar—often followed by, "I am going to pray about this." I myself have said, "Let me pray about this," when I really meant, "I need time to come up with more reasons why I refuse to do this but can blame God for it!"

Pray diligently for divine direction about your neighborhood. Ask for your heart to be prepared for ministry. Ask for a love for your neighbors. Ask for help mending broken picket fences and building new bridges between homes. Ask for front doors to be opened.

If you have pre-prayed, you are pre-pared.

Your decision to love your neighbor may not come with a peaceful, easy feeling. I had no "peace" with my decision to invite eighty-nine women over for coffee. Far from it! This commitment invited disruption and loss of time and fear and inconvenience and rejection. My peace came from knowing I was being obedient to the Lord's leading and that He was greater than all my fears.

> Your decision to love your neighbor may not come with a peaceful, easy feeling.

Love your neighbor. You don't have to be weird.
I promise, the reward is worth the risk.

# Next Best Steps

1. Have you ever felt like the devil was trying to get you down? What happened? How did you defend yourself?

2. List the attacks of discouragement you've experienced as you've read this book. Could this be a spiritual attack?

3. How do your own personal actions impede your progress in your neighborhood? When has God disciplined you like a loving Father? List one change you can make to take responsibility and move forward.

4. Recall a trial that has brought you closer to God. What did you learn about Him? What did you learn about yourself?

5. Who in your neighborhood needs grace today? How will you extend it to them?

6. Write a statement of your initial excitement and later fear about loving your neighbor. Circle the subject of each sentence: Is it you? God? Your neighbor?

# The Neighborhood Café

I created the Neighborhood Café based on my experience in my own neighborhood. You begin by hosting an Open House for your neighbors and friends, then invite them back for Bible study. The Neighborhood Café equips you for ministry, eradicates your excuses, prevents you from making the same mistakes I did, and helps you create new relationships in your neighborhood.

Please explore additional free resources at my website, www .howtoloveyourneighbor.com.

## Howtoloveyourneighbor.com

Visit www.howtoloveyourneighbor.com, where you can:

- Learn more about starting your own Neighborhood Café.
- Share your neighborhood story.
- Watch a video about my experience in my neighborhood.
- Browse tips and tools at the blog.

- Listen to my podcast.
- Download free tools.
- Like our Facebook page.
- Connect with me! I'd love to talk with you about your neighborhood.

Appendix B

# Additional Resources

These resources will help you provide powerful, effective ministry from your own front porch.

## Abundant Community
## www.abundantcommunity.com

The book and website *Abundant Community* asserts that we need our neighbors and a community to be healthy, produce jobs, protect the land, and care for the elderly and those on the margin. John McKnight and Peter Block state, "Our consumer society constantly tells us that we are insufficient and that we must purchase what we need from specialists and systems outside the community. We outsource our health care, child care, recreation, safety, and satisfaction. We are trained to become consumers and clients, not citizens and neighbors." This secular resource takes "a thoughtful look at how this situation came about, what maintains it, and the crippling effect it has had on our families, our communities, and our environment. . . . Block and McKnight recommend roles we can assume and actions we can take to reweave the social fabric that has been unraveled by consumerism and its belief that however much we have, it is not enough."

## Apartment Life
## www.apartmentlife.org

Apartment Life's mission is to transform the lives of apartment residents by fostering environments where residents can build authentic friendships and develop lasting community! Apartment Life is a faith-based, nonprofit organization that is motivated by the belief that every individual is created for community. Their CARES program is a community building and resident retention program that provides business value to apartment owners and management companies while making a lasting difference in the lives of apartment residents. The CARES program is carried out by a CARES Team (a married couple, family, or "team of two"). Once recruited, each CARES Team is placed into apartment communities to live onsite and work with the management team to build community and serve residents by doing things that flow naturally out of the Christian lifestyle—welcoming new residents, planning social events, and CARE-ing in times of need.

## Art of Neighboring
## www.artofneighboring.com

In the spring of 2010, twenty-one churches in the metro Denver area came together for a shared sermon series centered on neighboring. Their goal was to challenge the people in their congregations to be intentional in relationships with their literal neighbors. Their hope is that the people who are a part of this movement will move from strangers to acquaintances, then from acquaintances to relationship with the people who live closest to them. This movement continues to grow, both in Denver and in cities around the country as government and faith-based leaders launch their own neighboring movements. Jay Pathak and Dave Runyon wrote about their experience in *The Art of Neighboring* (Baker Books, 2012).

## Circle of Friends
## www.ourcircleoffriends.org

Circle of Friends Ministries is a nonprofit women's ministry that desires to encourage women to follow Jesus Christ through venues of radio, worship, conferences, and writing. They host "banner" events that reach out into communities such as simulcasts, retreats, and servant evangelism projects. They also assist local church women's ministry programs with event development and planning. Media technology is used as a venue to encourage women through Christ-focused music, devotional messages, and interactive discipleship/teaching.

## Girlfriends Café
## www.girlfriendscafe.org

Girlfriends Café is a coffee fellowship time for ladies that includes three components: enjoying some girlfriend time, participating in a fun activity, and listening to a testimony of how God is working in someone's life. During the evening, coffee, tea, hot chocolate, and cold drinks are provided along with a dessert of some type. This event can be accomplished in about ninety minutes. It is fast-paced and packed with constant interaction between the women. If you have been searching for a way to get to know and interact with other women in a positive atmosphere, this is for you. If your church would like to have their own girlfriends café, materials are available for purchase at the website.

## Facebook Groups
## www.facebook.com/groups

Facebook Groups are the place for small group communication and for people to share their common interests and express their opinions. Groups allow people to come together around a common cause, issue, or activity to organize, express objectives, discuss issues, post photos, and share related content. When you create a Group for your neighborhood, you can decide whether to make it publicly available for anyone to join, require administrator approval for members to join, or keep it private and by invitation only. New posts by a Group are included in the News Feeds of its members, and members can interact and share with one another from the Group.

## Lotsa Helping Hands
## www.lotsahelpinghands.com

Lotsa Helping Hands brings together caregivers and volunteers to help organize daily life during times of medical crisis or caregiver exhaustion in neighborhoods and communities worldwide. Caregivers benefit from the gifts of much needed help, emotional support, and peace of mind while volunteers find meaning in giving back to those in need.

## Mary & Martha
## www.maryandmartha.com

DaySpring Cards, a division of Hallmark that specializes in Christian cards and other products, offers a home party division called Mary & Martha. Mary & Martha features entertaining and hospitality items with an inspirational message and exclusive designs. Their products and tips give you the confidence that you can have people in your home without it being perfect, complex, or routine so you can focus on the main thing—the guests who enter your home. Mary & Martha Independent Consultants combine faith and work in a home party setting.

## Meetup
## www.meetup.com

Meetup is the world's largest network of local groups. Meetup makes it easy for anyone to organize a local group or find one of the thousands already meeting up face-to-face. More than nine thousand groups get together in local communities each day, each one with the goal of improving themselves or their communities. Meetup's mission is to revitalize local community and help people around the world self-organize. Meetup believes that people can change their personal world, or the whole world, by organizing themselves into groups that are powerful enough to make a difference.

## My Neighbor In Need
## www.myneighborinneed.org

My Neighbor In Need provides a nurturing, dignified way to connect individuals who have a specific need with those who wish to fulfill that need. They believe that every single person at one time in their life has had a need. For some, that time is right now! They also believe that each of us has the capacity, talent, and ability to help their neighbors in need. Finally, they believe that each of us can provide help because help comes in many different forms. You can establish My Neighbor In Need in your community by enlisting one person who can oversee the project and coordinate three to five volunteers who can dedicate twenty to twenty-five hours a week. Needs are verified before they are posted to a website. Partnerships with local media promote the project and needs.

## NBS2G
## www.nbs2go.com

Neighborhood Bible Studies are changing lives! NBS2GO is simply the packaging of ideas, resources, and inspiration of the NBS movement so that women everywhere feel encouraged and equipped to launch their own groups. Their dream is to see women around the world gathering their neighbors to study the Bible. Since neighborhoods are so central to our lives, they see them as the perfect setting to share Christ, to reach out to our neighbors with friendship, and to present the hope of the Gospel. Although each expression of neighborhood ministry is as different as each of us are, there are some common themes, elements, and resources that every woman can use along the way.

## Neighbor Brigade
## www.neighborbrigade.org

Neighbor Brigade establishes and mobilizes community-based networks of volunteers in New England to provide immediate and free assistance to neighbors experiencing sudden crises such as cancer treatment, illness, accident, or other tragedy. Neighbor Brigade transforms local communities into networks of support through which neighbors quickly mobilize to help other residents in emergency situations. It is a simple idea with tremendous impact in providing relief to those in crisis while strengthening the fabric of a community.

## Neighbourhood Prayer Network
## www.neighbourhoodprayer.net

This UK-based network offers tips and encouragement for anyone to get to know their neighbors. By partnering with churches and similar ministries, they aim to see every street in the UK covered in Christian prayer. They hope to encourage as many Christians as possible to not only pray, but get to know their neighbors. They ask Christians to pray for their neighbors, care for their neighbors, and share their faith. Subscribe to their free weekly email for helpful advice, current news, and testimonies from around the Network.

## Nextdoor
## www.nextdoor.com

Nextdoor is a private social network for you, your neighbors, and your community. It's an easy way for you and your neighbors to talk online and make all of your lives better in the real world. And it's free. Thousands of neighborhoods are already using Nextdoor to build happier, safer places to call home. Nextdoor's mission is to use the power of technology to build stronger and safer neighborhoods.

People are using Nextdoor to:

- Quickly get the word out about a break-in
- Organize a Neighborhood Watch
- Track down a trustworthy baby-sitter
- Find out who does the best paint job in town
- Ask for help keeping an eye out for a lost dog
- Find a new home for an outgrown bike
- Finally call that nice man down the street by his first name

## Praise and Coffee
## www.praiseandcoffee.com

Praise and Coffee began as a blog in 2007 by Sue Cramer. Praise and Coffee groups were launched in the following years. Their vision is to see women connect, encourage, and inspire one another through Praise and Coffee groups meeting in every state and across the world! Praise and Coffee groups encourage honest conversations that lead women to a better understanding of what Jesus did and how it affects our journey with Him every day. They encourage women to invite a few friends out for coffee and share life. Praise and Coffee is not supported by or affiliated with any church or denomination. Download instructions for starting your own Praise and Coffee group at the website.

## Q Place
## www.qplace.com

Q Place recognizes that there are many people in our culture who would appreciate the opportunity to interact with questions about God and the Bible in a supportive environment. Their mission is to mobilize people to start groups and equip them to become excellent facilitators. With time-tested guidelines and solid inductive resources, facilitators cultivate a healthy group process so that everyone in the group can come to conclusions at their own pace. Q Place comes alongside churches as advisors and coaches and enables them to create an effective, self-sustaining ministry. People have been drawn to Q Place because their inductive approach to learning allows them to interact with faith-related topics, which is especially important when people have doubts or major questions.

## Womensministry.net
## www.womensministry.net

Womensministry.net is a storehouse of ideas, resources, tools, and information exchange among Christian women and ministry organizations worldwide. They are passionate about empowering women's ministry leaders to initiate, nurture, and sustain vibrant transformational ministries for women. Subscribe to a free weekly email for tips on building teams, creating relationships, and being an empowered leader in your church or community. Search thousands of free articles for icebreakers and ideas for a gathering in your home, or join for premium, members-only content.

Visit www.howtoloveyourneighbor.com to discover new resources!

Appendix C

# Mapping and Demographic Websites

Use these sources to map your neighborhood, identify your neighbors, and pray for them by name. Then hit the streets and meet them in person!

## Google Maps
## www.maps.google.com

Google Maps is a web-mapping service provided by Google offering satellite imagery, street maps, and street view perspectives. Google Maps satellite images are not updated in real time; however, Google adds data to their primary database on a regular basis, and most of the images are no more than three years old.

## Bing Maps
## www.bing.com/maps

Bing Maps offers detailed street maps as well as a bird's-eye view that displays aerial imagery captured from low-flying aircraft.

Unlike the top-down aerial view captured by satellite, bird's-eye images are taken at an oblique, 45-degree angle. They show the sides of buildings, not just the roofs, and give better depth perception for geography. These images are typically much more detailed than the aerial views taken from directly above. Signs, advertisements, pedestrians, and other objects are clearly visible in many bird's-eye views.

## White Pages
## www.whitepages.com

Type your address into WhitePages.com, and records of your neighbors' names and addresses are instantly available on a Bing map. Previous owners associated with an address will also be shown. WhitePages was founded in 1997 with a single vision: to help people find, be found, and connect. WhitePages ingests billions of records every month from a variety of public sources and organizes that data by linking individual records to create an intricate contact graph of names, phone numbers, and addresses.

## Your Local Government Website
## publicrecords.netronline.com

Find the official state website, Tax Assessor's and Recorders' offices in your area using the Public Records Online Directory. Locate your own property, then use these public records to identify your neighbors' names and addresses. Although not every county and parish has data online, many have home pages, and where neither is available a phone number has been provided.

# Notes

## Chapter 1: The View From My Window

1. The She Speaks Conference derives its name from Proverbs 31:26 (NIV), "She speaks with wisdom, and faithful instruction is on her tongue." It is sponsored by Proverbs 31 Ministries. Visit www.shespeaksconference.com or www.proverbs31.org to learn more.

2. Matthew 22:39; Mark 12:31; Luke 10:27; Romans 13:9; Galatians 5:14; James 2:8; Leviticus 19:18

3. *Strong's Exhaustive Concordance: New American Standard Bible, Updated Ed.* (La Habra, CA: Lockman Foundation, 1995); Blue Letter Bible, "Strong's G1656—eleos," www.blueletterbible.org/lang/lexicon/lexicon.cfm?Strongs=G1656&t=NKJV.

4. Oswald Chambers, "How Will I Know?" *My Utmost for His Highest* (Grand Rapids, MI: Discovery House, 1992), October 10.

## Chapter 2: Welcome to Your Neighborhood

1. Aaron Smith, "Neighbors Online," Pew Research Internet Project, June 9, 2010, www.pewinternet.org/2010/06/09/neighbors-online.

2. Jed Kolko, "Love Thy Neighbor?" Trulia, October 24, 2013, www.trulia.com/trends/2013/10/love-thy-neighbor.

3. Ibid.

4. *Matthew Henry Bible Commentary—Luke 24*, BibleStudyTools.com, www.biblestudytools.com/commentaries/matthew-henry-complete/luke/24.html.

5. *American Time Use Survey Summary* (Washington, DC: U.S. Bureau of Labor Statistics, 2013), www.bls.gov/news.release/atus.t01.htm.

6. Ibid.

7. Aaron Smith, "Older Adults and Technology Use," Pew Research Internet Project, April 3, 2014, www.pewinternet.org/2014/04/03/older-adults-and-technology-use/.

8. "Facebook may be the largest 'country' on earth by 2016," Royal Pingdom blog, February 5, 2013, http://royal.pingdom.com/2013/02/05/facebook-2016.

9. Sam Laird, "Social Networks: Are They Eroding Our Social Lives?" *Mashable*, April 25, 2012, http://mashable.com/2012/04/25/social-networks-study.

10. "Social Networking Eats Up 3+ Hours Per Day for the Average American User," MarketingCharts, January 9, 2013, www.marketingcharts.com/online/social-networking-eats-up-3-hours-per-day-for-the-average-american-user-26049.

11. Stephen Marche, "Is Facebook Making Us Lonely?" *The Atlantic*, April 2, 2012, www.theatlantic.com/magazine/archive/2012/05/is-facebook-making-us-lonely/308930.

12. Ana Mendez-Villamil, "Millennials Heart UGC," CrowdTap, April 9, 2014, http://blog.crowdtap.it/2014/04/millennials-heart-ugc-infographic; Ipsos MediaCT, *Social Influence: Marketing's New Frontier*, March 2014.

13. Aaron Smith, "6 New Facts About Facebook," Pew Research Center, February 3, 2014, www.pewresearch.org/fact-tank/2014/02/03/6-new-facts-about-facebook.

14. Stephen Marche, "Is Facebook Making Us Lonely?"

15. Ibid.

16. Ibid.

17. Kate Loveys, "5,000 Friends on Facebook? Scientists Prove 150 is the Most We Can Cope With," *Daily Mail*, January 24, 2010, www.dailymail.co.uk/news/article-1245684/5-000-friends-Facebook-Scientists-prove-150-cope-with.html.

18. Moira Burke and Robert Kraut, "Growing Closer on Facebook: Changes in Tie Strength," Research at Facebook, April 26, 2014, https://research.facebook.com/publications/216645348525231/growing-closer-on-facebook-changes-in-tie-strength-through-site-use.

## Chapter 3: Home Sweet Home

1. Jed Kolko, "Love Thy Neighbor?" Trulia, October 24, 2013, www.trulia.com/trends/2013/10/love-thy-neighbor.

2. Dr. Danny Avula, "Dependence Isn't a Dirty Word," TEDxRVA Talk, May 9, 2014, www.youtube.com/watch?v=7cDeMjvrFjU&feature=youtu.be.

3. Charles R. Martin, "Extraversion or Introversion," *The Myers and Briggs Foundation*, www.myersbriggs.org/my-mbti-personality-type/mbti-basics/extraversion-or-introversion.asp. Adapted from Charles R. Martin, *Looking at Type* (Gainesville, FL: Center for Applications of Psychological Type, 1997).

4. Hilarie Stelfox, "Talking Point: The Rise of Loneliness in 21st Century Britain," *The Huddersfield Daily Examiner*, November 30, 2013, www.examiner.co.uk/news/west-yorkshire-news/talking-point-rise-loneliness-21st-6355301.

## Chapter 4: Don't Be Weird

1. Divya Raghavan, "Most Diverse Cities in America," nerdwallet.com, October 1, 2013, www.nerdwallet.com/blog/cities/lifestyle/most-diverse-cities-in-america.

2. Megan Johnson Shen, Megan C. Haggard, Daniel C. Strassburger, Wade C. Rowatt, "Testing the Love Thy Neighbor Hypothesis: Religiosity's Association With Positive Attitudes Toward Ethnic/Racial and Value-Violating Out-Groups," *Psychology of Religion and Spirituality*, November 2013, 294–303; "Do Religious People Love Their Neighbors? Yes—Some Neighbors, Study Finds," Phys.org, January 24, 2014, http://phys.org/news/2014-01-religious-people-neighbors-yessome.html#jCp.

3. Personal conversation with Rockie Naser, used by permission.
4. "Six Reasons Young Christians Leave Church," Barna.org, September 28, 2011, www.barna.org/barna-update/millennials/528-six-reasons-young-christians -leave-church.
5. "There are 7 Mountains of Influence in Culture . . ." 7 Cultural Mountains, www.7culturalmountains.org.

## Chapter 6: It's All Spiritual

1. Charles Forelle, "The Snap Judgment on Crime and Unemployment," *The Wall Street Journal*, April 15, 2009, http://online.wsj.com/articles/SB12397 4939828118493.
2. John McKnight and Peter Block, *The Abundant Community: Awakening the Power of Families and Neighborhoods* (San Francisco: Berrett-Koehler Publishers, 2010), 2–3.
3. Annie Lowrey, "Income Gap, Meet the Longevity Gap," *The New York Times*, March 15, 2014, www.nytimes.com/2014/03/16/business/income-gap-meet-the-longevity-gap.html?_r=0.
4. Alice Park, "Change Your Neighborhood, Improve Your Health," *Time*, October 20, 2011, http://healthland.time.com/2011/10/20/change-your-neighborhood -improve-your-health.
5. Barbara L. Fredrickson, *Love 2.0: Creating Happiness and Health in Moments of Connection* (New York: Hudson Street Press, 2013), 56–57.
6. Lynn E. Alden and Jennifer L. Trew, "If It Makes You Happy: Engaging in Kind Acts Increases Positive Affect in Socially Anxious Individuals," *Emotion*, February 2013, 64–75.
7. L. Congdon, "Be Kind—and Unwind," *Martha Stewart Living*, May 2014, 126–129.

## Chapter 7: Unwrapping Your Gifts

1. Larry D. Gilbert, *How to Find Meaning and Fulfillment Through Understanding the Spiritual Gift Within You* (Elkton, MD: Church Growth Institute, 2005).

## Chapter 8: Say What?

1. Charles H. Spurgeon, "A Sermon (No. 3438)" (sermon, Metropolitan Tabernacle, Newington, CT, December 24,1914), www.blueletterbible.org/Comm/ spurgeon_charles/sermons/3438.cfm?a=938036.

## Chapter 9: Martha Unleashed

1. J. Vernon McGee, *Thru the Bible with J. Vernon McGee, Vol. 4* (Nashville: Thomas Nelson, 1983), 443.

**Amy Lively** is a writer and speaker who provides tips, tools, and teaching about loving our neighbors without being weird, offensive, or pushy. Amy draws from her own experience knocking on her neighbors' doors and leading a women's neighborhood Bible study. She is passionate about helping people identify their unique ministry gifts and use them in their community. She has a degree in practical ministry and oversees communication to the congregation and the community at Life Church Ohio. Amy, her husband, and their daughter live in Lancaster, Ohio, with a holy dog and an unsaintly cat. Learn more at www.howtolove yourneighbor.com.